Managing change in schools

Developing Teachers and Teaching

Series Editor: **Christopher Day**, Professor of Education, University of Nottingham.

Teachers and schools will wish not only to survive but also to flourish in a period which holds increased opportunities for self-management – albeit within centrally designed guidelines – combined with increased public and professional accountability. Each of the authors in this series provides perspectives which will both challenge and support practitioners at all levels who wish to extend their critical skills, qualities and knowledge of schools, pupils and teachers.

Current titles:

Managing change in schools

Patrick Whitaker

Open University Press
Buckingham · Philadelphia

5-3-00

Open University P
Celtic Court
22 Ballmoor
Buckingham
MK18 1XW

and

1900 Frost Road, Suite 101
Bristol, PA 19007, USA

First Published 1993
Reprinted 1994

A catalogue record of this book is available from the British Library

Library of Congress Cataloging-in-Publication Data

Whitaker, Patrick.
    Managing change in schools / Patrick Whitaker.
        p.   cm.
    Includes bibliographical references and index.
    ISBN 0-335-09382-5 – ISBN 0-335-09381-7 (pbk)
    1. School management and organization – Great Britain.
    2. Educational change – Great Britain.   I. Title.
    LB2900.5.W49   1993
    371.2'00941 – dc20   92-23836
                                                              CIP

Typeset by Graphicraft Typesetters Ltd, Hong Kong
Printed in Great Britain by St Edmundsbury Press Ltd, Bury St Edmunds, Suffolk

For Claire

That which transforms things and fits them together is called change; that which stimulates them and sets them in motion is called continuity. That which raises them up and sets them forth before all people on earth is called the field of action.

The I Ching or *Book of Changes*
Richard Wilhelm translation rendered into English by Cary F. Barnes
(Routledge and Kegan Paul, 1978)

Contents

Series editor's introduction

This is a much overdue and important addition to the literature on managing change in a world which the author believes is characterized by accelerated change, ambiguity and turbulence, and in which schools and other organizations are in continual critical – and often stressful – interaction with their physical and social environments. Drawing upon writings of visionaries and practitioners from within and outside the education and business communities and writing from experience of practice, Patrick Whitaker focuses upon the human factors in managing change, challenging leaders to adopt an evolutionary perspective. Only through focusing upon individual motivation, interaction and behaviours, and a balance of consideration for the task and the person will long term goals be achieved. The book focuses upon leadership, organizational cultures and the management of change and is an expression of the vision and practice of its uniquely talented author. It adds to the growing literature on the importance of 'educative' leadership which challenges mechanistic orthodoxies of change and development in which managers control, direct and supervise. In this perspective, prime functions of leaders are to create conditions for human growth and development and develop collaboration cultures which are built around personal empowerment and the active involvement of all workers. This book is essential reading for all leaders who recognize the importance of taking time to think, reflect and plan in order to increase their own capacity and that of the teachers and schools to learn, adapt, and manage change successfully.

Christopher Day

Preface

This book is about change and how we manage it. It sets out to explore the world of rapid and accelerating change in which education is now placed and examines the range of challenges facing those involved in the management of schools.

The book has two key purposes. First, to explore the phenomenon of change and its place in our lives and secondly to consider the practical implications for managing it. It approaches this exploration from an individual standpoint but also at the organizational level, focusing on the fundamental challenge of leadership in the collaborative setting. It is not a book concerned with specific issues of change such as the National Curriculum or Local Management of Schools, these are dealt with in detail elsewhere, it is about change as an ever-present feature of our lives and a constant challenge to organizations.

Chapter 1 is concerned with the social and political context within which education is currently placed and offers a personal view of the issues involved. Chapter 2 considers a range of perspectives on change and the future, setting the challenges facing schools in the wider context of world events. Chapter 3 is about the individual and examines the processes involved in personal change and development. Chapter 4 examines the dynamics of change and considers the nature of professional learning. Chapter 5 focuses on the sort of leadership that is required to manage change successfully. Chapter 6 explores the vital issue of organizational culture and the creation of an appropriate climate for change. Chapter 7 provides some frameworks of the change process and offers practical strategies. Chapter 8 considers some longer term challenges of the future for those currently in senior position in schools and for those who will follow in the years to come.

The book has grown out of a strong commitment to the work of teachers and schools and from a fascination with organizations and how they work, in particular with how they can be developed to enhance and channel the enormous and often ignored potential that people bring with them to work. The ideas expressed in the book have emerged and developed in recent years through work undertaken throughout the country with teachers involved in the management of their schools. Their contribution has been paramount.

I should like to express some personal and special thanks. To Chris Day with whom so many of the ideas in the book have been developed in courses, conferences and workshops over the past ten years, for his constant enthusiasm and companionship. As the series editor he has been more patient than I have deserved. To Harold Heller who not only gave me so many opportunities to develop approaches to the management of change but shared so many of his own distinctive and original ideas. To Dave Hicks who has provided constant support and encouragement and whose practical advice has been especially valuable. To John Skelton, who as the publisher, helped me to confront my own uncertainties and boosted my confidence when I most needed it. To Frank McNeil, Jane Reed and Geoff Southworth for so many stimulating conversations about education and change. I am also particularly indebted to Keir Whitaker who has throughout the process of writing this book listened to my ideas, shared his own experience, challenged my thinking and assisted my struggle for understanding.

Acknowledgements

The author is grateful for the following permissions to reproduce copyright material:

Basil Blackwell for material on the Third Corner, from A. Mant (1983) *Leaders We Deserve*; Cassell for the use of the cultural matrix, from S. Murgatroyd (1988) 'Consulting as counselling: The theory and practice of structural consulting' in H. Gray *Management Consultancy in Schools*; Harper Collins for the table on The Paradigm Shift in Learning, from M. Ferguson (1982) *The Aquarian Conspiracy*, and for the figure on leadership style, from K. Blanchard, P. Zigarmi and D. Zigarmi (1987) *Leadership and the One Minute Manager*; Prentice Hall for the material on the cultural web, in G. Johnson and K. Scholes (1983) *Exploring Corporate Strategy*; Kogan Page for the five features of leadership, in J. Adair (1990) *Not Bosses but Leaders*; Penguin Books Ltd for the material on trust, from C. Handy (1983) *Understanding Organizations*; the James Robertson for the five scenarios, J. Robertson (1983) *The Sane Alternative*.

The educational context

The changing legal framework

It is an indication of the nature and pace of change that there has been more educational legislation since 1980 than in the whole previous history of education. The deliberate decision by recent governments to intervene into areas previously regarded as the prerogative of the teaching profession perhaps indicates something of the insecurity experienced nationally about the nature of state funded education in a fast changing world. We have witnessed an increasingly disputatious public and professional debate about how the nation's children should be educated, but far from tackling the problems of designing education for a rapidly changing world, the debate seems only to have succeeded in fuelling differences of ideology between those wishing to preserve traditional notions of schooling and those wanting to advance radically the progressive momentum begun in the 1960s.

One significant impact of legislation has been the tightening of the bureaucratic nature of schooling. It is now defined by an enormous quantity of legislation and regulation, and a decade of local and national interventions have put into place a range of complex new systems and procedures. The key question is the extent to which all this legislation and regulation will achieve the hopes raised for it. Changes in educational practice tend to come from practitioners themselves rather than through regulation, and legislation can be seen as a somewhat desperate attempt to respond to the confusion created by rapid and accelerating change. In this sense the intervention of national government can be regarded as a symptom of change rather than a cause of it, producing extra flurries of activity at national, local and school level.

Innovation

While legislation and regulation defines and determines the structure and organization of the schooling system, much of the innovation in classroom practice and curriculum derives from the discoveries, insights and experiences of the practitioners. One of the significant features of state education is the uneasy tension between national policy makers and grass roots practitioners. The nature of professional specialism tends to inhibit the government from intervening in areas which they have no training and expertise to affect.

The key challenge for teachers has always been one of how to achieve optimum learning in a group of pupils in a classroom setting. No amount of tinkering with governing bodies or admission limits will fundamentally affect that challenge, unless it is to change the principle fixed assumption of the system – that learning is best achieved when pupils are arranged in groups of about thirty with one teacher in a classroom.

Perhaps the most powerful influence on what happens in the classroom has been tradition. The structures and systems laid down from the very earliest attempts to organize schooling, as opposed to personal tutoring, have survived virtually intact to the present day. This is not a tribute to the effectiveness of the early models of classroom pedagogy as much as an indication of the strength and power of tradition. Many of the great educators – Rousseau, Dewey, Montessori have been concerned with the individual learner. Much of the history of schooling has been characterized by an attempt to give pupils an individual experience in a group setting. It is only very recently that the potential of the group itself to assist and promote learning has really been grasped and experimented with.

Most of the changes in classroom practice, particularly in the nursery and infant stages of schooling have been brought about by good practitioners working with curiosity about how their pupils learn best. Such teachers have demonstrated an ability to change as a result of significant experience. Good practice therefore has always been held up by teacher trainers, school inspectors and headteachers as something to emulate. Teaching has thus become subject to fashions and bandwagons. Good practice by highly effective teachers, working from a deep theoretical understanding of what they are doing, has been held up for emulation by others who have not been informed of the experience and theory underpinning it.

Far from indicating a failure among teachers to discern appropriately, it emphasizes the enormous complexity of the processes involved in learning and teaching and demonstrates a concern among teachers to find ways of managing an extremely complex and challenging task – that of creating optimum learning in large groups of different, individualistic and differentiated learners.

Key considerations for educational change

Eventually the education system will find its own way out of its organizational difficulties. To do this successfully, however, it will need to move out
and away from its traditional reliance on permanency and the perpetuation
of traditional institutions. Reforms to education have tended to focus on two
key areas – the structure of schooling and the content of the curriculum.

The structure of schooling

A catalogue of structural changes – selective secondary education, comprehensive schools, an increased span of compulsory attendance, the creation
of new local education authorities and the introduction of new types of
schools – have been attempts to create conditions in which the learning of
pupils can be more effectively achieved. Yet in themselves, these changes
have not satisfied the considerable hopes raised for them.

The content of the curriculum

Compared with modifications to the structure of schooling, those directed
at the curriculum have been immense. Over the past thirty years vast resources have been allocated to curriculum research and development. First,
the Schools Council and later the School Curriculum Development Commit-
tee were formed to coordinate development and dissemination of new ideas
in the fields of curriculum and examinations. Now with these bodies long
gone there is little evidence that the prestigious projects of the early 1970s
have radically modified the curriculum in either primary or secondary schools.
The plethora of reports by Her Majesty's Inspectorate (HMI), the Department of Education and Science (DES) and government committees of enquiry remain largely unread by the majority of those involved in the
day-to-day teaching in our schools.

The Education Reform Act 1988 has radically changed the process of
curriculum development and reform, imposing on schools a national programme of content based on core and foundation subjects, four key stages
of learning, programmes of study and attainment targets. In addition a
national system of assessment and testing has been introduced with external
examinations being conducted at the ages of 7, 11, 14 and 16.

Some of the most significant features of this change have been the difficulty of imposing an untested model on pupils and the challenge of producing a definitive set of targets relevant in a fast changing world. Major
changes to the core subjects have had to be made even before the foundation subject curriculum has been agreed. Two large bureaucracies have
been created to devise, implement, monitor and evaluate this new system
but it is difficult to make a case that they will succeed in helping the process

of schooling become the liberating and deeply satisfying experience it should
be for its participants.

The process of learning

As a result of these preoccupations with structural alterations and curriculum reform, educational development has failed to take sufficient account
of a significant third way to progress. This may be conceptualized as the
climate and culture of schooling. It relates to those considerations which are
essentially the human factors of the system:

- personality
- relationships
- interactions
- values
- behaviour
- experience

These elements contribute in significant ways to the creation of satisfactory conditions for learning and teaching and to the capacity of pupils
to acquire and develop knowledge, skills and qualities in the collective
setting of the classroom.

It is important to note that as management and organizational theory has
developed in recent years, increasing consideration has been given to the
concept that workplaces are essentially organizations of people, brought
together to pursue specific aims and purposes. Current experience indicates
that if the needs and motivation of the workforce are satisfactorily related
to the agreed purposes of the organization then effectiveness and efficiency
are likely outcomes. The evidence from a detailed examination of well-run
companies is that long-term profitability is best achieved where management processes are built around personal empowerment and the active
involvement of all workers.

In recent years theories of management have affected the ways that schools
are run. Management training in education is increasingly concerned to
present a model of leadership based on participation, and headteachers are
encouraged to involve all staff in decision making and the day-to-day
management of the school. It is becoming increasingly important to see
leadership as a process of harnessing the potential of individual participants,
not controlling and prescribing their behaviour. The process of human
endeavour is increasingly recognized as equal in importance to considerations
of task and product. Commercial organizations are quickly learning that
survival in a fast changing world depends very much on the creativity,
flexibility and resilience of staff. Management is adapting from its concern
with bureaucracy, maintenance and efficiency to a determination to maximize
the abilities of people by attention to the needs and aspirations that each

participant brings with them into the organization. This involves the creation of a management culture in which individuals feel more able to release their energies to shared visions and objectives. In other words, process is concerned with an enhanced view of human potential. It is concerned to create conditions in which the people involved can grow and develop and become more than they currently are.

So too in the process of learning, survival in a fast changing world may well depend upon the ability of pupils to develop skills in adaptation, flexibility, cooperation and imagination. The process of schooling needs to be seen as a key focus in the management of change. It has been largely ignored in the recent concerns to improve the quality of education. Obsession with structure and content has resulted in a dangerous neglect of the learning process, perhaps the most important factor contributing to successful educational change and development.

Factors affecting educational change

Improvement

In the struggle to manage change and achieve improvement, educators are faced with a range of challenges and difficulties. Three issues particularly tend to feature in debates about change.

Competition

It is unfortunate that so much of what happens in education is affected by the competitive ethic – being brighter than someone else, getting higher marks, achieving a landmark first. It applies in the rivalry between the state and private sectors, and now within the state sector itself as Local Management of Schools links school survival with pupil recruitment. One of the common polarized arguments hinges on the belief by one side that competition is the essence of progress and the belief by the other that competition merely sustains inequality of opportunity and inhibits successful learning. A concern with rivalry – of winning, or at least not losing – can cloud attention to the more fundamental purposes of education.

Recrimination

Not succeeding in your learning has become a cause for blame. It is not so long ago, and certainly in the memory of some readers of this book, that getting things wrong resulted in some form of physical punishment. Apart from learning by fear to avoid punishment, a sense of inadequacy is instilled and low confidence in learning abilities created when we do not always get things right first time. An obsession with deficits has long been a preoccupation in the educational system and moulding us from our natural selves into a 'correct' being has been a priority for many schools.

Reform

Much change in education has had a reform element about it. The assumption that changing the structure of schooling is the way to ensure improved learning is still the belief of many politicians. While improvement is constantly needed it is sad that many of the reasons forwarded for wishing to improve are so connected with tangential issues – to be better than other countries, to prove experts wrong, to increase the competitiveness of British industry or because standards are different than they were fifty years ago. In all this there seems a reluctance to grasp the essential fact – that the world is different than it was, and is changing fast. For an educational system to be in tune with change it needs to be flexible, adaptable and responsive to constantly changing circumstances and needs.

The obsession with current deficits and difficulties does nothing to advance the idea of an educational system for a changing world. It merely deepens prejudices, further polarizes positions and keeps the debate focused on what exists now rather than on the visions of what it will need to be like in ten or twenty years time.

The solutions currently being introduced assume that the only issues to take account of are the ones that have always been taken account of – those that seemed to be appropriate to a world that has passed. Imagination about change only stretches to considerations about more or less of what we already have. The rush to discover panaceas creates a tendency to retrieve discarded orthodoxies from the past such as streaming, exclusively didactic instruction and single technique approaches to reading.

Nowhere in the current round of reform is there present the notion that the most appropriate change is continuous and systematic improvement, in which change is seen as a constant process of building and developing, rather than an event to be engaged in with great energy when things have got really bad. If schools cannot be trusted to change for themselves then intermittent flurries of activity will be necessary. As the pace of change in the world accelerates these flurries will become more necessary and more insistent, and sadly, increasingly dysfunctional.

Rigidity

One of the difficulties facing those charged with the management of schools is the rigid context for education envisaged by the reformers. Educational change is approached in strictly rational terms as a choice between opposing alternatives, only one of which is right. This manifestly fails to realize that education and learning is characterized by complexity and an infinite range of variables. Simple solutions must be at worst wrong and at best partial.

The great debate is not a fundamental exploration of ideas and possibilities about issues of learning and teaching, but a bitter and protracted argument about who is right and who is wrong. Proposals for a Royal Commission are turned down probably because the learning that might accrue from such an exploration could be embarrassing to entrenched positions and ideologies. Once polarized on party political lines a non-judgemental and truly independent search for ideas and possibilities becomes impossible. In addition, such explorations take time, which reforming governments do not have. Changes have to be instant, enforced and backed by centralized power.

This perpetuates the pendulum process in education, with swings one way and then the other. Either the pendulum is pushed by the political weight of legislation and regulation or eased in the other direction as proponents begin to feel their job is done and opponents seize the day.

This binary structure inhibits creative exploration and becomes an issue of winning or losing the argument. The learning process becomes the victim of politics. We are so fixed into the pattern of binary thinking that change outside this polarized dynamic becomes incomprehensible and ridiculous.

Those responsible for the direction of educational policy need to realize what an increasing number of commercial organizations have realized – that survival and development in a fast changing world depends upon simultaneity rather than exclusion. Polarized patterns of thinking automatically exclude certain variables and include others – the 'either/or' approach to change. Creative solutions will undoubtedly include some elements of both positions – divergence and variation will demand it. There needs to be sufficient variety of policy and practice to make development possible. Ashby's Law of Requisite Variety (Garratt 1987) suggests that for an organization to survive and develop there must be sufficient difference within it to allow it to cope with change. The pursuit of monolithic structures will produce too much similarity thus reducing the ability of the system to learn and adapt to a rapidly changing environment.

As the centralized and increasingly bureaucratized system becomes more rigid it will be necessary for individual schools to have the courage of their convictions to plan for what they believe to be the best interests of pupils, parents and the community. The Grant Maintained option may not be pursued in order to support a political principle, but to avoid it.

Polarization

One of the most dispiriting features for those involved in the running of schools is that the debate about education is conducted in a climate of dispute and discord. This sets up stresses and tensions which themselves have a debilitating effect on the process of change itself. Because issues are polarized and arguments rehearsed there is no need to ask fundamental questions about what the basic purposes of schooling in a fast changing world are, nor to involve participants in the answers and solutions.

A worrying characteristic of the debate has been the increasing tendency to denigrate educational specialists – 'experts' – those who dare to offer an opinion based on first-hand experience and systematic study. It is easy to scoff at those whose influence you fear, and convenient to marginalise ideas and interpretations that jeopardize your own position.

This sometimes forces the specialists to increase the vehemence of their arguments, to claim more for their research than is reasonable and to extend their generalizations into territories for which they were not destined. This further fuels the polarization within the educational community itself creating a warfare of ideologies and entrenched positions. Just as in warfare it is the innocent and uninvolved who become the victims.

On the other hand, there is no escaping the fact that education is a legitimate political issue. It is naive to hope for a day when education will be freed of political intervention. Those charged with the management of educational institutions need to be clear about this political reality and develop a capacity to work within its sometimes painful clutches.

One way to do this is to listen to the quieter voices, particularly those of the learners themselves. It is significant that in all the documentation of the National Curriculum not one page of it has been written and offered to the pupils. If anyone needs to know the targets for learning it is those faced with achieving them.

Education is a synthesis – a bringing together of knowledge, ideas, possibilities and practicalities. Its very essence is experience and the meaning that is construed through reflection on it. There is very little reflection in the current debate among the protagonists. Successful change requires reflection as well as reaction, thinking as well as doing and vision and imagination as much as intellect and belief.

The inheritance factor

Despite the pressures to change the schooling system, the strength of traditional orthodoxy is immense. As schools struggle to adapt to accelerating change, it is useful to consider the 'inheritance factor'. This can be described as the tendency to cling to structures from the past.

One of the most powerful tenets of schooling systems throughout the world is the notion of the single teacher in relation to multiple learners. It is implicit in the architecture, organization, staffing and funding of schools. There appears to be an unshakeable belief that not only is this the cheapest way to educate – it is the only way. While there has been a gradual reduction in the pupil–teacher ratio there does not seem to have been any attempt to challenge the basic concept.

So we perpetuate a schooling system developed out of economic necessity and inspired by the factory principle that human resources were costs rather than resources and as such the most expendable ingredient in the process.

A second inheritance is the predominance of factual knowledge in the learning process. While primary education has seen more change and development than other phases of schooling, even the most progressive of institutions have offered a curriculum which would compare closely with models that existed before compulsory education. Today with the added factor of the National Curriculum there is a chilling familiarity about the opening episode in Charles Dickens' *Hard Times*:

> Now what I want is Facts. Teach these boys and girls nothing but Facts. Facts alone are wanted in life. Plant nothing else and root out everything else. You can only form the minds of reasoning animals upon Facts: nothing else will ever be of service to them.
>
> (Dickens 1961)

Relating this to current debates is the question of what is so dangerous about 'everything else'? Perhaps it is that ideas, questions, values and concerns are damaging to the status quo, that learners will get ideas above their station. Which is of course exactly what happened. Mass literacy not only gave access to the Bible but to *Das Kapital*; and we know the history of the twentieth century. Now the books that children should read are prescribed by the National Curriculum. Just as eastern Europe is releasing itself from two generations of prescription, the forces of change in this country seemed determined to anchor the developments in the past instead of the future.

Separation/integration

It is important to clarify some of the competing concepts that contribute to the confusion that so often attends the debates and discussions about education. In an attempt to clarify, the following working definitions are offered:

1 *Education* a continuous process in which instruction, guidance and teaching is offered to learners by others.
2 *Schooling* the process of organizing education within institutions through legislation and regulation.
3 *Learning* the self-managed process of acquiring and developing knowledge, understanding skills, values, and attitudes.
4 *Teaching* the process of providing instruction, guidance and support for prescribed learning within the legal framework of schooling.

These distinctions emphasize the essential difference between learning as a largely self-managed and self-directed aspect of human growth and development, and the deliberate structuring of teaching within institutional settings.

One of the unfortunate effects of formalized educational systems is the growth of the assumption that education only happens in schools and is delivered through formal instruction. Although the narrow association of learning with schooling is a difficult one to shift there have been significant developments in recent years which have helped to develop a much wider and more integrated concept of education and learning.

Research and development in the field of adult education has produced a range of exciting new insights and methodologies. The need to look beyond the somewhat restricted notions of pedagogy – specifically the art and science of teaching children, has produced androgogy – the art and science of helping adults to learn. This significant conceptual innovation has helped to move the definition of education from one about teaching to one of assisting learning. The principles of adult learning are based on a number of critical assumptions about the characteristics of adult learners and the ways they differ from those of child learners:

1 An adult's self-concept moves from one of being a dependent personality towards one of being a self-directed human being.
2 Adults accumulate a growing reservoir of experience that becomes an increasing resource for learning.
3 An adult's readiness to learn becomes oriented increasingly to the development tasks of social roles.
4 An adult's time perspective changes from one of postponed application of knowledge to the immediacy of application thus shifting the learning orientation from one of subject centredness to one of problem.

(Knowles 1983)

Twenty years after this important theoretical breakthrough it is interesting to consider to what extent these four assumptions highlight important characteristics of learners irrespective of age. Day and Baskett (1982) have challenged the distinctiveness of these apparent differences, suggesting that many of the principles upon which adult learning is based are also relevant to pupils in schools. What is needed, they argue, is a re-examination of our understanding of the nature of pupil learning in the light of these insights.

Developments in adult learning theory have supported and enabled major innovations in education. Perhaps the most significant of these was the establishment of the Open University which broke totally with tradition, espousing the almost heretical assumptions that degree level learning could be embarked upon without any prior educational qualifications, did not require a face-to-face relationship with a teacher and could be managed through self-directed activity in the home. Building on this highly successful breakthrough the notion of open learning is now an established part of educational theory and practice.

The notions of continuing and community education have also challenged many of the traditional assumptions upon which the educational system is built. First, that education has to be age specific. In community schools and colleges, pupils learn alongside adult members of the community to mutual benefit, creating a different and more liberating classroom culture. The inspiration of The University of the Third Age in Toulouse has demonstrated that learning capacity does not diminish with age but can be applied successfully well beyond the assumed retiring age. The spread of self-help groups has demonstrated the enormous learning potential of the group, especially when it is based upon principles of involvement, participation and equal rights and responsibilities.

The emphasis on experiential and inductive learning has spread beyond the world of adult education, pervading schools from the top via the Training and Vocational Education Initiative (TVEI). These innovations mirror practice in the early years of education with its strong foundation of activity, involvement and experience within them.

These movements are helping to break down the notion of separation between schooling and learning. Within schools this has led to a growing concept of partnership between teacher and taught with a more facilitating and enabling relationship as a key variable in creating educational success for pupils. Ideas of 'the negotiated curriculum' have been a feature of some secondary schools for some time and the gradual breaking down of the curriculum/pastoral dichotomy is creating a new climate for innovation and change.

Into these important developments has intervened the Education Reform Act. Not only has this upset the equilibrium of continuous change and development through school based innovation, it represents a challenge to many of the insights and understandings that have influenced school development, and re-established the polarity between traditional and progressive, hard and soft, tough and tender approaches.

Those involved in the management of schools need to be aware of the force of these traditions and the deeply ingrained nature of these orthodoxies. They have become basic cultural assumptions held by successive generations of those who have experienced the schooling process. Perhaps those who have succeeded in the system see no need to change what apparently worked for them. Those who have failed have been led to blame themselves for the failure and not to question the system's capacity to provide a differentiated and individual experience.

What we are now witnessing in the debate about the nature and future of schooling is a curious amalgam of clinging to traditions and letting go of the past. This cultural ambivalence has all the signs of a society deeply confused about how to adapt to a world that is different than it was even one generation ago and which is changing at an increasingly fast rate. The process of managing change invokes this confusion, producing an uncomfortable tension between preservation and alteration.

Rapid change creates two characteristics which exacerbate feelings of confusion and discomfort – uncertainty and messiness. The desire to know what is likely to happen, what particular outcomes change will produce and how personal adaptation will be coped with are deep needs in most of us. The desire to live in an organized world of clear categories, tidy systems and ordered functions is also strong. The trouble is that the world is now characterized by turbulence, systemic stress, boundary blurring and temporary expediency. In attempting to create a culture of change it is necessary for educational managers to help their colleagues to develop a psychological metabolism sturdy enough to cope with increasingly higher levels of disorder and uncertainty. The leadership of change requires the capacity to work at both the levels outlined at the beginning of the chapter – the personal and the organizational.

2
Perspectives on change

Introduction

The purpose of this chapter is to produce a range of views and perspectives about the future in terms of current trends and tendencies. In a world where change is an increasingly constant feature it is useful to place our personal and professional experience against a wider backdrop and to raise awareness of some ways of thinking about the future.

When we contemplate the future we often imagine it will be much like the present although with more of some aspects and less of others. James Robertson (Robertson 1983) has suggested that we have a choice of futures – both ones to imagine and ones to work for. He poses five scenarios, each assumed by some people to be the only realistic view.

1 Business as usual

The future will be much like the present and the past. While change will happen, the main problems of the world will not alter significantly. People will continue to conceive the problems in much the same way as they always have and use current methods and ideas for solving them.

2 Disaster

This scenario suggests that the world is on a catastrophe course with little alternative to increasing unrest, famine, pollution, poverty, crime and that the doom scenario is a nuclear war. It is a view attractive to pessimists.

3 Authoritarian control

A variety of left- and right-wing versions of this can be distinguished. The scenario suggests that only authoritarian control can avert the dangers facing the world and that it is necessary to curb individual freedom in order properly to enforce law and order and distribute resources fairly. It is a scenario appealing to those with an authoritarian, controlling and dominating temperament, who identify strongly with the ruling class and have a low opinion of the governed.

4 Hyper expansionist

This suggests that the solution to the world's problems lies in accelerating the super industrial drive of western society and making greater investment in science and technology – space colonization, nuclear power, genetic engineering and artificial intelligence. This scenario tends to appeal to ambitious, competitive people.

5 Sane, humane, ecological future

Instead of forcing an acceleration of change we should shift direction towards a balancing of people with nature. The priority is to learn to live supportively with one another on this small and overcrowded planet.

Robertson's work is concerned with promoting the fifth scenario as the only one likely to sustain life and improve its quality.

It is also interesting to note how these five scenarios are reflected in the ways schools are run, and the ways that professional cultures reflect different perspectives on the educational future:

The stable state (business as usual)

Keep your heads down, all the fuss will pass over and we will soon be able to carry on much as we always have.

Doom and gloom (disaster)

We are witnessing the gradual disintegration of the educational system as we have known it. Politicians are committed to these changes and there is not much we can do about it.

Tight management (authoritarian control)

What schools really need is tight management with clearly defined structures and systems. It requires central direction of the curriculum and more powers to governing bodies to control the professionals. A tough, no non-sense approach to both management and teaching is most likely to restore a proper sense of direction and purpose and to restore achievement to former levels.

Innovate (hyper expansionist)

A high tech, science-based education will help us to survive and to make sure that we have a proper supply of scientists and technicians to manage the future. Huge investment in information technology is necessary both to create more efficient management but also to revolutionize the process of learning.

Human collaboration (sane, humane, ecological future)

Instead of reforming what we have, we need to transform the way we manage education. This is necessary in order to maximize the huge potential that learners bring with them to the schooling process and to release the enormous creativity and skill that is currently locked up within the teaching force.

Most organizational cultures are extremely complex, containing elements of all the above. It is naive to expect any organizational culture to be consistent when the world around is so volatile, but it is important to note how in certain situations of challenge we can find ourselves displaying these various responses to change and the future.

Evolution

Those concerned to help in the development of an educational service which is future focused may feel that the imposition of a National Curriculum is inhibiting the capacity of schools to introduce programmes geared to a world in which constant change and uncertainty are the norm.

One of the key assumptions upon which traditional orthodoxy in education has been built is that teaching in schools is concerned with the transmission of knowledge, knowledge that will remain valid throughout our lives. Alfred North Whitehead observed over fifty years ago that such an approach would only work if the time-span of major cultural change was greater than the life span of individuals. But now:

> We are living in the first period of human history for which this assumption is false . . . today this time span is considerably shorter than that of human life, and accordingly our training must prepare us to face a novelty of conditions.
>
> (Whitehead 1931)

For those managing schools this novelty focuses both on the functions, purposes and processes of learning for tomorrow's world, and on how to create management cultures able to respond quickly and creatively to constant change.

It is important to develop a sense of historical proportion and an appreciation of how our current dilemmas and concerns relate to evolutionary history. The planet we are struggling to save and develop is five billion years old. If we were to compress the evolutionary process over this vast period into one single year then:

March	the first single cells appear
November	multicellular organisms evolve
13 December	dinosaurs
15 December	mammals
26 December	dinosaurs extinct
31 December 11.49pm	homo sapiens
11.59pm	civilization
11.59.58	industrial era

In the last two seconds before midnight we have caused:
● serious damage to ecosystems
● major loss of biodiversity
● genocide of indigenous peoples
● nuclear waste for 250,000 years.

(Milbrath 1989)

It is not easy for educational managers to cultivate such an evolutionary perspective. The pressure to resolve the dilemma between the urgent and the important tends to give school management a 'here and now' feel. Long-term thinking and planning is becoming an indulgence rather than a necessity in the constant struggle to keep pace with the present. One of the paradoxes created by rapid change is that managers will need to operate almost simultaneously in the present and in the future, constantly relating current realities to future needs and possibilities.

The extended present

Not only do educational leaders and managers need to have an appreciation of the significance of current evolutionary challenges in order to build schools geared to change, they need to help pupils and students to develop an altogether different conceptual approach to the past, present and future.

Elise Boulding, an American educator, has developed a useful concept – the 200-year present. She reflects that when we consider evolutionary history we see great sweeps of time in which individual human events can seem insignificant. The present has a fleetingness in that it has gone before we know it. Between these two, she says, there is a medium range of time that is not too long for immediate comprehension but which has an organic quality very relevant to the present moment:

> This medium range is the 200 year present. That present begins 100 years ago today, on the day that those among us who are centenarians were born. Its other boundary is the hundredth birthday of the babies born today. This present is a continuous moving moment, always reaching out a 100 years in either direction from the day we are in. We are linked with both boundaries of this moment by the people among us whose life began or will end at those boundaries, five generations each way in time. It is our space, one that we can move around in directly in our own lives and indirectly by touching the lives of the old and young around us.
>
> (Boulding 1988)

In the year in which National Curriculum history is being introduced into schools this offers a novel and attractive perspective of our place in evolutionary history. It offers the interesting notion of a change raft, moving with the flow of time. As it leaves behind the most remote events of the past it takes on new hopes for the future. It offers a perspective on change that is comprehensible and accessible to the young and introduces an important and much neglected feature – a concern with the future.

There is evidence of a general incapacity to take the future seriously. Experiments conducted annually over a period of years suggest that a reluctance and an incapacity to contemplate the future in a serious and considered way is deeply resisted. When graduate parents of pre-school children were asked what they anticipated the world would be like when their children were 21 the answer was: 'We would rather not think about it. We hope things won't be worse than they are now.' Parents of undergraduate students were asked what their retirement plans were (15 to 20 years ahead): 'We would rather not think about it.' Undergraduate students were asked to think ahead to their own retirement years and the responses were: 'We will be dead by then.'

The significant feature is that over the forty-year period in which these questions have been annually posed, the nature of the responses has altered little (Boulding 1988).

There is an element of psychological helplessness about these views of the future. Because we lack the concepts and tools to undertake such a contemplation in anything other than speculative daydreaming, education will have a vital part to play in helping to sustain an interest and optimism with the future. It is significant that young children seem to demonstrate nothing of the fear exhibited by their parents:

I hope that in the future there will be no more war and hunger and the world will become green and everybody will care to make it better and the world will unite again.

My hopes for the future are to have a happy life and to live for a long time and have a nice family. And that my cat and goldfish will live for a long time.

One of my fears for the future is that I'll get highjacked in a plane, another is that I'll get stuck in an elevator.

Another world fear is that the atmosphere will get polluted so that we cannot live any longer.

(Hicks 1993)

The Global Futures Project, based at Bath College of Higher Education is providing a positive focus on the role of the future in children's learning. The project is designed to help pupils and teachers to:

1 Develop a more future oriented perspective on their own lives and events in the wider world.
2 Identify and envision alternative futures which are just and sustainable.
3 Exercise critical thinking skills and the creative imagination more effectively.
4 Participate in more thoughtful and informed decision making in the present.
5 Engage in active and responsible citizenship, both in the local and global community, on behalf of present and future generations.

In *Education for the Future: a Practical Classroom Guide* (Hicks 1993) a rationale is set out listing pupil outcomes in relation to knowledge, attitudes and skills:

1 pupil motivation
2 anticipating change
3 critical thinking
4 clarifying values
5 decision making
6 creative imagination
7 a better world
8 responsible citizenship
9 stewardship

These could well form the basis for a programme of professional development for educational managers. There is an urgency to this work if the future blindness uncovered by Boulding in her research is to be overcome.

Whatever we do, the present we are now living through will become an extremely well-documented past. In fifty years time educators and historians will look to the documents of the time to see how well we are adapting a schooling process to a fast changing world. School Development Plans will become subjects of research degree dissertations. It is interesting to speculate what these researches might tell future generations about our current awareness of change processes and of our capacity to work imaginatively and creatively with them.

A fable

A powerful insight into the nature of rapid and accelerating change and the challenges facing those charged with managing it is provided by the following fable:

The Lily and the Farmer

A farmer had a big pond for fish and ducks. On the pond was a tiny lily. The tiny lily was growing. It was doubling in size every day.

'Look', said the people to the farmer, 'You'd better cut that lily. One day it'll be so big it'll kill all your fish and ducks.'

'All right all right,' said the farmer, 'But there's no hurry. It's only growing very slowly.'

The lily carried on doubling in size every day. 'Look,' said the farmer several days later, 'the lily is still only half the size of the pond. No need to worry yet.'

The next day the farmer was very surprised.

(Richardson 1983)

Paradigm shifts

In his book *The Structure of Scientific Revolutions*, Kuhn (1970) introduces the notion of a paradigm shift – a profound change in the thoughts, perceptions and values that form a particular view of reality. He illustrates the paradigm shift within the scientific community by describing what happens when a particular scientist deserts the rules of the paradigm and makes a discovery that does not fit within it. Since it does not fit it has to be proved wrong. But other scientists also discover puzzling anomalies which further strain the orthodoxy. The only way out of the crisis is the creation of a new paradigm. This involves the incorporation of a principle which was present all along but has remained either 'undiscovered' or ignored. The new paradigm is received with scepticism and some hostility and its ideas are attacked. Some established scientists remain unconverted even when confronted with overwhelming evidence. When the number of new adherents reaches a critical mass, a collective paradigm shift can be said to have occurred.

Kuhn's conceptual breakthrough in our understanding of the process of change is important because it challenges the view that all change is a smooth and natural process. It highlights the difficulties faced by those confronting the resistance of vested interest. Since the whole notion of the paradigm is a rigid tightening around specific beliefs and ideas, change must be seen as the painful and protracted process of reinventing, reordering and redefining. This is the hallmark of a world determined to develop itself on certainty. Every time the paradigm is redefined there develops a belief that here at last is the final correct solution.

What we are now witnessing in the world of change is the attempt to create a paradigm which is characterized by the acceptance of temporariness rather than certainty, by possibility rather than unlikeliness and integration rather than exclusion. Such a paradigm is a departure from the idea of singular solutions to problems to an appreciation of complex and multiple solutions. It is a way of thinking that recognizes that in apparent dichotomies there are the seeds of new connections and partnerships. 'Both . . . and . . .' becomes a more exciting alternative to 'either . . . or . . .'

The following sections of the chapter take the idea of the paradigm shift out of the scientific community into a wider world view. They outline a variety of perspectives on change from people who have researched and worked in the field. They offer ideas and possibilities as well as noting significant trends and tendencies.

The Aquarian Conspiracy

In her book *The Aquarian Conspiracy*, Marylin Ferguson looks at issues of personal and social change during the 1970s and 1980s. In the light of Kuhn's work on the paradigm shift she offers the notion of hidden pictures in children's books and magazines. A casual look at the country scenes shows trees, a pond, some fencing and animals in the fields. The instructions ask you to look more closely – for objects you had no reason to believe were there. But suddenly you begin to pick out the camouflaged objects that lie concealed.

> Nobody can talk you into seeing the hidden pictures. You are not
> persuaded that the objects are there. Either you see them or you don't.
> But once you have seen them, they are plainly there whenever you
> look at the drawing. You wonder how you missed them before.
> (Ferguson 1982)

She uses this as an example of the many minor paradigm shifts we are constantly experiencing as we grow up: 'The opening up of a new paradigm is humbling and exhilarating; we are not so much wrong as partial, as if we had been seeing with a single eye. It is not more knowledge, but a new knowing.'

In terms of how we change, Ferguson suggest four basic ways:

1 *Change by exception* Our belief system remains intact but allows for a few anomalies: 'the exceptions that prove the rule'.
2 *Incremental change* This occurs a bit at a time and we are not aware that we have changed: 'I was almost right, but now I'm right'.
3 *Pendulum change* This is the periodic abandonment of one closed and certain system for another: 'I was wrong before, but now I'm right'.
4 *Paradigm change* This happens when insights allow information to come together in a new form that refines and integrates previous understanding. It allows for different interpretations from different perspectives at different times: 'I was partially right before, and now I'm a bit more partially right'.

This provides a useful insight into how change can be managed in schools. Much of the success will depend upon the extent to which transformational change is developed as a cultural assumption within the organization.

In the section of her book entitled 'New Ways of Learning', Ferguson articulates one of the key paradoxes of the schooling system: 'As the greatest single social influence during the formative years, schools have been the instruments of our greatest denial, unconsciousness, conformity and broken connections.' She raises the idea of pedagogic illness – the educational equivalent of iatrogenic or doctor caused illnesses. Learning disabilities, she suggests, are caused by the separatist and often alienating experiences of many students in classrooms.

In her proposal for a new educational paradigm she suggests that the key lies in looking to the nature of learning rather than to the curriculum and methods of instruction. To succeed in satisfying the needs of a fast changing and uncertain future she proposes a list of elements in the paradigm shift as shown in Table 1.

In noting an innate conservatism and resistance to change in western educational systems, she points to some of the essential differences between schools and commercial organizations.

> Schools are entrenched bureaucracies whose practitioners do not compete for business, do not need to get re-elected or to attract patients, customers, clients. Those educators who would like to innovate have relatively little authority to change their style.

It will be interesting to see to what extent recent legislation, in introducing a greater competitive element into the schooling process, succeeds in increasing the authority of internal innovators to change their style.

Table 1 Paradigm shift in learning

Old paradigm assumptions	New paradigm assumptions
Emphasis on content, acquiring a body of 'right' information, once and for all.	Emphasis on learning how to learn.
Learning as a product, a destination.	Learning as a process, a journey.
Hierarchical and authoritarian structure. Rewards conformity, discourages dissent.	Students and teachers see each other as people not as roles.
Relatively rigid structure, prescribed curriculum.	Flexible structures, varied starting points, mixed learning experiences.
Age related learning.	Integration of age groupings. Learning not age specific.
Priority on performance.	Priority given to the self-concept as the key determinant of successful learning.
Emphasis on external world. Inner experience considered inappropriate in school setting.	Use of the pupil's inner experiences as contexts for learning.
Guessing and divergent thinking discouraged.	Guessing and divergent thinking encouraged as part of the creative process.
Emphasis on analytical, left brain thinking.	More emphasis on right brain, intuitive activity.
Classroom designed for efficiency, convenience.	More concern for learning environment – colour, comfort, personal space and privacy.
Education seen as an age related social necessity.	Education as a lifelong process and only partially related to schools.
Teacher as instructor and imparter of knowledge.	Teacher as a learner too, learning from the pupils.

The implicate order

In the search for meaning and understanding, an increasing number of theoretical scientists are searching for connections beyond the confined worlds of their disciplines. It is part of a recognition that the mechanistic world view based on reductionism – the idea that all complex phenomena can be reduced to their constituent parts, so providing insight and understanding – can no longer provide insights into a world at the edge of chaos. The distinction between mind and matter proposed by Descartes produced a dualism that supported the separation of humanity from nature, thus sanctioning the manipulation and exploitation of the natural world. By applying the same mechanical laws that seemed to explain the working of the universe to living organisms separated from their environment, a wedge was driven into the notion of harmonious coexistence. The Newtonian synthesis of the universe as one huge mechanical system operating to exact mathematical laws spread to the human sciences including theories of organizations. The idea that in human affairs, cause and effect are exact has led to confusion, misunderstanding and misdirection.

David Bohm is a physicist who has challenged the mechanistic paradigm. His work has shown that sub-atomic particles have a tendency to behave harmoniously with perfect synchronicity even though separated in space and apparently unconnected. Two particles although occupying completely different parts of the universe have been shown to respond to each other as if they were parts of a whole. This led Bohm to propose the theory of the implicate order – that all of reality is enfolded in all of its parts.

In the enfolded order, space and time are no longer the dominant factors determining the relationship of dependence or independence of different elements. Rather, an entirely different sort of basic connection of elements is possible, from which our ordinary notions of space and time, along with those of separately existent material particles, are abstracted as forms derived from the deeper order. These ordinary notions in what is called the explicate or unfolded order, which is a special and distinguishing form, are contained within the general totality of all the implicate order (Bohm 1980).

The significance of this concept to our work in education is that integration is a more powerful and enhancing force in human affairs than separation, and that we need to pursue vigorously the sense of connectedness – building structures and processes which emphasize interrelatedness and participation rather than division and detachment. This involves structural and cultural changes in our schools, both in the curriculum, in the processes of learning and in the activities of management.

Ilya Prigogine, the Belgian Nobel physicist has discovered a vital element within this implicate order that has important implications for the management of change. His theory of dissipative or open structures notes that complex structures are connected at many parts and in many different ways.

The system is in constant flux since the connections can only be sustained by a flow of energy. Entropy or disorder is created by the breaking down of old structures by newly forming ones, but the dynamics of self-organization results in self-renewal, adaptation and evolution. The Cartesian perspective – human systems as machines – has encouraged us to believe that organizations are reasonably straightforward and predictable. The insights of Bohm and Prigogine present a view of infinite complexity and constant flux within which there is flowing wholeness in which instability and transformation are constantly interweaving. As managers we must break free from the idea that we can determine or design organizational cultures and respect the powerful but subtle interplay of complex human forces at work. Leadership needs to be seen more as a sensitive response to climate and conditions than the application of strategies and techniques.

Third Wave

One of the first writers to bring concepts of the future to public attention was Alvin Toffler. *Future Shock*, written 20 years ago, charted the manifestations of rapid change in western industrial society. His phrase 'future shock' was coined to describe an increasing and sometimes overwhelming disorientation caused by living in a society characterized by constant and rapid change.

In the book, he charts a number of key themes. He notes the death of permanence, the emergence of transience, the novelty of new circumstances, the need for diversity and the limits of adaptability. Above all he stresses the urgency of the search to discover strategies for survival. Now twenty years after publication, these phrases have an increasingly telling relevance in our lives.

Toffler identifies two main constituents of change: the rate of change and the direction of change. On the first of these he states:

> When we speak of the rate of change, we refer to a number of events crowded into an arbitrarily fixed interval of time. Thus we need to define the 'events'. We need to select our intervals with precision. We need to be careful about the conclusions we draw from the differences we observe. Moreover, in the measurement of change, we are today far more advanced with respect to physical processes than social processes. We know far better, for example, how to measure the rate at which blood flows through the body than the rate at which a rumour flows through society.
>
> Even with these qualifications, however, there is widespread agreement, reaching from historians and archaeologists all across the spectrum to scientists, sociologists, economists and psychologists,

that, many social processes are speeding up – strikingly, even spectacularly.

(Toffler 1971)

While change occurs at different rates and paces, its omnipresence is now a constant feature of our lives. Attitudinal change may lag behind technological and scientific change, creating great difficulties in reconciling old values to new circumstances. This attitudinal lag is a major challenge in organizations creating a dissonance between change itself and our capacities to make sense of it. The increasing attention given to the incidence of occupational stress testifies to the often overwhelming sense of turbulence.

In terms of the direction of change, Toffler points to the need for a new psychological metabolism designed to cope creatively with the constant emergence of novel conditions. He coins the phrase 'adhocracy' to describe an approach to life and work that is altogether less rigid and more flexible than we have been socialized to – a sort of social and psychological nomadism, requiring us to adapt quickly, change direction and move on.

Toffler's perspective for the 1980s is called *The Third Wave*. In it he suggests that we are in the midst of a new civilization, bringing with it new family styles, new ways of working, loving and living; a new economy; new political conflicts and above all an altered consciousness. Some are successfully attuning themselves to this emergent civilization while others, 'terrified of the future, are engaged in a desperate, futile flight into the past and are trying to restore the dying world that gave them birth' (Toffler 1980).

This new civilization, he suggests, is the key to understanding the years ahead:

It is an event as profound as the First Wave of change unleashed ten thousand years ago by the invention of agriculture, or the earthshaking Second Wave of change touched off by the industrial revolution. We are the children of the next transformation, the Third Wave.

(Toffler 1980)

One of the keys to the Third Wave, Toffler suggests, lies in breaking the code – the hidden design that enabled the industrial paradigm to exert such a powerful grip on our ways of living and thinking. He identifies six interrelated principles that have programmed our behaviour and which need to be modified if we are to make our way successfully in the world of tomorrow.

1 *Standardization*   The social obsession with similarity, categorization and uniformity.

2 *Specialization*   The belief in the separation of knowledge, expertise and labour.
3 *Synchronization*   An economy and social system dependent on fixed time scales and patterns – clock driven work, people paid for how much time they put in rather than for what they do – peak holiday periods and rush hours.
4 *Concentration*   Of people – huge sprawling cities, schools, prisons, hospitals, giant corporations and monopolies.
5 *Maximization*   An infatuation with bigness and growth. Big is best and might is right – the tallest skyscraper, the largest factory, the biggest shopping mall.
6 *Centralization*   Central control of political decision making, the judiciary and state bureaucracy.

Already we can see significant changes in each of these six areas. The transition from the Second Wave to the Third will be messy and sometimes painful. Each of the six principles apply to the management of schools and there is much value in considering them in terms of the extent to which the school is inclining towards or moving away from them.

As industrial/technological societies move inexorably towards the Third Wave it will be vital to develop new forms of management and leadership to accompany them. The paradigm shift in management is already well under way and among the Third Wave companies and the new wave of smaller businesses have come bold experiments in the organization and management of work. For Toffler, leadership with its strong directional connotation will be a more important idea than management, which perhaps smacks of maintenance, the status quo and the stable state. He warns, however, that it will be necessary to challenge two particular misconceptions about leadership.

First, he argues, it will be necessary to release ourselves from the myth of authoritarian efficiency which attaches so much importance to the small group at the top of organizational hierarchies to provide all the direction, supply all the answers, and exercise all the control. This has the effect of minimising the capacity of others in less senior positions to offer their abilities and creativity to the search for effective ways forward.

Secondly, we must avoid sustaining the belief that because certain styles of leadership have worked in the past they will do so in the present or future. Broader notions of leadership and management need to be developed, that look beyond status, authority and formal power as the significant elements in organizational structure. The coordination of imagination, the release of skill and creativity and the collaborative involvement of all those with a stake in the organizational enterprise will become the abiding requirement in the changed and changing future.

The Turning Point

Another view of the move from one wave of change to another is provided by Fritjof Capra in *The Turning Point*. He too detects a new order emerging. In particular he charts the emergence of a new scientific paradigm and a move away from the reductionist and mechanistic world view. Like Toffler, he observes the turning point to be a change from emphasizing the studying of things in isolation to the importance of taking account of relationships, contexts and wholes. Like Bohm, he sees reality as only understandable in terms of integrated wholes whose properties cannot be reduced to those of smaller units.

The concept of the turning point is used by Capra to highlight the inexorability of the emerging order. While there may be no turning back, there will certainly be forces of resistance and restraint. It is interesting to consider the issues dealt with in Chapter 1 in the light of this idea. For those involved in managing schools the forces unleashed through these shifts in social, cultural and scientific thinking will have strong repercussions. Managing schools, like any other organization, will be highly challenging. It will involve stress, frustration and confusion, but it will also be fascinating, sometimes exhilarating and never dull.

The emergence of a new scientific paradigm is mirrored in other fields – economics, psychology, medicine, social welfare and health care. This integrative tendency in the paradigm shift reflects a growing understanding that we need to see the world as a living system whose components are interconnected and interdependent. It is a notion that the scientist James Havelock has entitled *The Gaia Principle*.

The implications for organizations and institutions are clear:

1 That the school, or any other institution, is an organism in continual and critical interaction with its physical and social environment.
2 That an organization cannot be understood and managed successfully by identifying discrete functions and activities and managing them separately.
3 That a healthy organization is a dynamic system of interacting parts and that dysfunction in one particular part has an effect on the whole.
4 That the management of parts needs to contribute to a thrust towards synthesis and integration.

It is against the complexity of this background that the work of schools is set. The challenge to those managing schools is one of holding simultaneously an awareness of global developments while attending to the local and immediate. These varied perspectives emphasize the need to develop flexible ways of thinking about the present in relation to a past which is gone and an uncertain future which is yet to come. Many of the youngest pupils now in schools will live well into the later stages of the next century. They will need both the intellectual capacity to cope with increasingly rapid change and the practical skills and abilities to adapt quickly to ever new situations and circumstances.

The personal dimension

Personhood

A vital part of the paradigm shift outlined in the previous chapter is an enhanced view of personhood and human potential. One of the key contributing factors to this enhanced view has been the emergence over the past fifty years of humanistic psychology with its concern for the fully functioning person. The key pioneer was Abraham Maslow, who by asking about the psychology of the healthy and happy person sought to go beyond a preoccupation with personality dysfunction and the limitations imposed by attending only to behaviour, to discover a more comprehensive understanding of the human condition. In *Motivation and Personality*, Maslow (1970) set out his theory of the hierarchy of needs, the concept of self-actualization and important insights into the nature of happiness, love and learning. His pioneering work laid the foundations for further research and developments which have found practical expression in counselling, psychotherapy, self-help groups and the assertive alternative in interpersonal relationships.

It was Carl Rogers who led the way in translating Maslow's ideas into practicalities. He took Maslow's concept of self-actualization as the pinnacle of the needs hierarchy and placed it in a broader context:

> The mainspring of creativity appears to be the same tendency which we discover so deeply as the curative force in psychotherapy – man's tendency to actualize himself, to become his potentialities. By this I mean the directional trend which is evident in all organic and human life – the urge to expand, extend, develop, mature – the tendency to

express and activate all capacities of the organism, or the self. This tendency may become deeply buried under layer after layer of encrusted psychological defenses, it may be hidden behind elaborate facades which may deny its existence; it is my belief however, based on my experience, that it exists in every individual, and awaits only the proper conditions to be released and expressed.

(Rogers 1967)

One of the exciting developments in management theory and practice is the way that the notion of self-actualization is now being recognized in organizations and there is a new emphasis on the processes necessary to enhance human potential and capability – in other words to create the right conditions to release the actualizing tendency in all individuals, whether it be in families, schools, business organizations or in society as a whole.

History has demonstrated the enormous capacity human beings have to adapt and change in the face of the most fearful threats to survival and well-being. Humanistic psychology has helped to highlight the conditions in which change can be accomplished. The notion of safe psychological conditions is a vital one in the management of organizational change. More attention than ever before needs to be given to building organizational cultures that nourish self-esteem, build confidence, extend capability and increase motivation.

Theories X and Y

One of the most useful contributions to our understanding of organizations has been provided by Douglas McGregor, who in *The Human Side of Enterprise* (1960), highlighted the powerful effect that assumptions about personhood can have on work and motivation. McGregor posed two contrasting sets of assumptions about people in organizations, referred to as Theory X and Theory Y.

Theory X

People dislike work and try to avoid it. They have to be bribed, coerced and controlled and even threatened with punishment to perform adequately. Most people lack ambition, prefer to be led and wish to avoid responsibility. By nature people are resistant to change.

Theory Y

People do like work and don't have to be forced or threatened. If allowed to pursue objectives to which they are committed most people will work

hard and not only accept responsibility, but actively seek it. People have a
natural ability to change and adapt.

Managers and leaders proceeding from a Theory X position will tend to
build management structures and systems designed to: direct the efforts of
staff; control their actions; modify their behaviour to fit organizational needs.
They will also adopt interpersonal behaviour towards staff that is characterized by: persuasion; reward or punishment; instruction and command.

Managers and leaders who espouse Theory Y assumptions will tend to
build management structures and systems designed to: make it possible for
people to develop; seek responsibility; take risks; set ambitious targets and
challenges.

Clearly these are polarized positions but they do help us to place our
own experience within a powerful theoretical framework (see Figure 1).

For many of us, past experience in families, schools and the workplace
has been – unless we are exceptionally lucky – predominantly of the Theory
X kind. As a result of this, part of our career path into senior positions may
be motivated by a desire to avoid the controlling forces of Theory X being
exerted on us, and perhaps also to be amongst a smaller group in society
who hold power to control others. An important element in the development of managers and leaders is a capacity to develop an awareness of the
way that Theory X experiences have affected us and formed our behavioural
tendencies as managers. For many, the greatest challenge is balancing an
intellectual commitment to Theory Y with an experience that has conditioned
us in the dynamics of Theory X.

A less polarized view of people and work has been offered by Schein
(1980) who argues that complexity is the key characteristic of people and
that they tend not to behave consistently and predictably. No single style of
management can be regarded as relevant to all situations. What is needed
is behaviour appropriate to the needs and circumstances of varying
situations.

This emphasis on complexity is helpful in that it echoes the paradigm
shift already referred to. One of the problems of traditional management
practice has been an assumption of simplicity – that consistency and predictability in human affairs can be relied upon by leaders. As we become
more attuned to notions of complexity, uncertainty, unpredictability and
untidiness in human affairs we will learn to realize the importance of choice
and appropriateness in the face of differing circumstances and situations.

It is important to recognize the power of assumptions when a new job
is taken on. The new colleagues we work with, particularly those in junior
positions are likely to assume that any procedures or behaviours you adopt
are motivated by the same assumptions and reasons as your predecessor.
If you follow a Theory X manager and wish to inculcate a Theory Y culture
you may be disappointed and frustrated to find that new colleagues greet

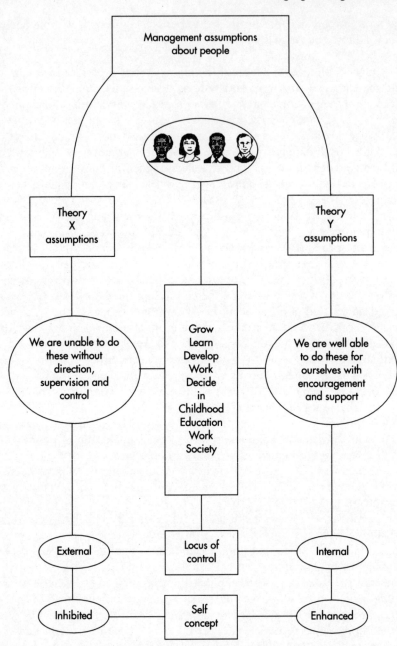

Figure 1 Management assumptions about people

your suggestions with some scepticism and mistrust – they may well assume that it is yet another device to control and contain them. To gain support it is necessary to overcome this powerful inheritance factor first by explaining your beliefs, concerns, assumptions and expectations and then making your interpersonal style as consistent as possible with these.

Toxic pedagogy

Figure 1 sets out a view of experience in relation to the assumptions that other people have held about us and about their role in the relationship. The formative influences for early experience cannot be underestimated in building understanding of why people behave as they do. In two powerful studies of early life and upbringing Alice Miller offers forceful and sometimes startling insights into the experiences of children in the often perilous journey from birth to adulthood.

In *For Your Own Good* (Miller 1987a) she examines the sources of violence within ourselves and the way these are encouraged by orthodox child rearing practices. She challenges the way in which successive generations have rationalized punishment and coercion as being for the child's 'own good' and charts the consequent costs in later life with diminished capacity for compassion and humanity. She cites the popular child rearing manuals of the nineteenth and early twentieth centuries in which parents are exhorted to do all within their power to 'break the will of the child' so that vital spontaneity and exuberance are properly inhibited, controlled and checked – the child thus developing a sober obedience and subservience. These manuals convey the belief that parents are always right and that 'every act of cruelty, whether conscious or unconscious is an expression of their love . . .' In a society increasingly alarmed by 'child abuse' Miller observes:

> Child abuse is still sanctioned – indeed, held in high regard – in our society as long as it is defined as child rearing. It is a tragic fact that parents beat their children in order to escape the emotions stemming from how they were treated by their own parents.
>
> (Miller 1987a)

She coins the phrase 'poisonous pedagogy' to describe the processes by which the potential of children and their actualizing tendency is contained, inhibited and sometimes crushed during the process of upbringing.

In *The Drama of Being a Child* (1987b), Miller shows how many children, by adapting themselves to the needs and ambitions of their parents, lose the ability to experience and express their true feelings and become out of touch with their real selves. Both these studies illustrate so graphically the Theory X structure at the root of our society – beginning in the parent–child relationship, extended in school, structured in the workplace and replicated in society.

The tradition of domineering and coercive leadership has deep roots in our own experience and in the traditions of parenthood, schooling and the organization of work. The paradigm shift is a movement away from this constraining dynamic towards a more enriching and liberating experience based on a deep respect for human potential and dignity, and a determination to create the best possible conditions for human growth, development and expression.

In a different way, Seymour Papert (1980) has provided insights into our positive experience as learners. He observes that children hold theories of the world that are coherent even though they may contain what adults would describe as 'false positions' as well as true ones. These theories, he says, enable children to take up temporary positions and meanings in order to make their way step by step in the world, each new step offering new experience which creates new meaning. Such theories are spontaneously 'learned' by all children in the pre-school years through a process which schools should envy:

> It is effective (all children get there), it is inexpensive (it seems to require neither teacher nor curriculum development), and it is humane (the children seem to do it in a carefree spirit without explicit external rewards and punishments).

Ultimate success in the formal learning process, he argues, depends upon our capacity to catch 'cultural seeds' – ideas stemming from the cultural environment which capture the imagination, form visions of possibility and motivate courses of action. It also involves a capacity to struggle with 'cultural toxins' – those ideas that plant a sense of failure within the self-concept. Using the example of mathematics he says:

> If people believe firmly enough that they cannot do maths, they will usually succeed in preventing themselves from doing whatever they recognize as maths. The consequence of such self-sabotage is personal failure, and each failure reinforces the original belief. And such beliefs may be most insidious when held not only by individuals but by an entire culture.

If the balance between cultural seeds and toxins weighs too heavily to the latter then 'learning disengagement' results. We begin to give up on learning, believing that it is too hard for us and we cannot do it. Eventually deficiency becomes identity: 'I don't have a head for figures,' 'I'm tone deaf,' 'I'm not well coordinated.'

Education, Papert suggests, has little to do with explanation and everything to do with engagement – or 'falling in love with the material'. Our capacity for growth and development is inextricably linked to the captivation of our awesome imaginations and to key aspects of our surrounding culture: to the steady growth of a sense of self-belief and possibility and to opportunities for practical exploration and experience.

It would seem then that the climate for change has much to do with our capacity for 'natural learning' and the extent to which the learner has optimum control of the learning experience. It also involves deliberate attention to the cultural seeds and cultural toxins.

Multiple intelligence

One of the obsessions of the education system is intelligence, and the debate about inheritance and environment continues. An enhanced perception of human potential requires that we develop a more holistic view of intelligence and its contribution to human achievement and personal effectiveness. Some interesting alternative definitions are emerging.

In *Inside Organizations* (1990), Charles Handy offers a working list which has several different types of intelligence:

Logical those who can reason, analyse and memorize.
Spatial those who can discern patterns in things and create them.
Musical those who can sing, play or make music of all sorts.
Practical the person who can pull a carburettor to bits but might never be able to spell the word or explain how they did it.
Physical the footballers, athletes and dancers among us.
Intra-personal the sensitive people who can see into themselves, the quiet perceptive ones.
Inter-personal those who can make things happen with and through people.

This offers an altogether new and richer view. As Handy observes:

> It is the tragedy of much of our schooling that we are led to think that logical intelligence is the only type that matters. Any observation of our friends and colleagues in later life will prove that the other intelligences are at least as important, if not more so.
>
> (Handy 1990)

We should, he argues, train ourselves not to ask how intelligent people are, but which type of intelligence do they have the most of?

The traditional view of intelligence emphasizes 'cleverness', mental agility and intellectual strength. During recent years a more balanced view has begun to emerge with an enhanced view of human intelligence. Denis Postle (*The Mind Gymnasium*, 1989) describes four types of intelligence:

1 Emotional intelligence
   • radiating warmth
   • awareness of own feelings

- sensitivity to feelings of others
- creating harmony and goodwill
- dealing with emotional issues openly
- empathizing with the experience of others

2 Intuitive intelligence
- 'gut' feelings
- hunches
- speculating about the future
- using imagination
- willingness to take risks
- capacity for change

3 Physical intelligence
- concerned with fitness and health
- enjoyment of physical activities
- pride in manual skills and dexterity
- sensible and balanced diet
- love of the outdoors
- good at household tasks

4 Intellectual intelligence
- reasoning
- problem solving
- analysis
- calculation
- handling information
- abstract ideas

Personal effectiveness draws on all four of these intelligence types and it is important not to over-value intellectual capacities at the expense of the others. Increasing evidence suggests that managers are perceived by others as effective when they behave sensitively in interpersonal situations, have a capacity to handle emotional situations well and are seen to be able to relax and enjoy a full and satisfying life outside the workplace.

A third view considers intelligence in the context of leadership and change in educational institutions. Management and leadership capability can be considered in relation to three distinct but interrelated areas of intelligence: professional intelligence; personal intelligence; managerial intelligence.

1 Professional intelligence

This is the type of intelligence we acquire and develop through professional training and experience. It generates qualities, skills and knowledge of a specialist and technical nature, specific to particular occupations and professions. Engineers have a different sort of occupational intelligence from nurses and lawyers. This type of intelligence is often the key focus in job related training within organizations.

2 Personal intelligence

This is an intelligence acquired and developed through the process of socialization. It generates personal qualities, skills and knowledge that enables us to develop and sustain relationships. It determines the capacity to get on well with other people in both professional and social settings.

Until fairly recently personal intelligence rarely featured in the formal educational process although it is constantly referred to by adults in the socializing of the young. Although it is crucially important in management it has rarely been the subject of training and development. It is often our relationships with others that cause our most difficult and emotionally painful moments. It is not surprising then that the additional pressures that work involves can increase the challenge and stress in our own relationships. Success in the management role requires us not only to be aware of this but to improve our own qualities, skills and knowledge in order to manage our relationships effectively and sensitively.

3 Managerial intelligence

This is an intelligence needed to work with and through other people. The following classification of managerial abilities provides a useful starting point for consideration:

1 Creating
   - having good ideas
   - finding original solutions to common problems
   - anticipating the consequences of decisions and actions
   - employing lateral thinking
   - using imagination and intuition

2 Planning
   - relating present to future needs
   - recognizing what is important and what merely urgent
   - anticipating future trends
   - analysing

3 Organizing
   - making fair demands
   - making rapid decisions
   - being in front when it counts
   - staying calm when the going is difficult
   - recognizing when the job is done

4 Communicating
  - understanding people
  - listening
  - explaining
  - written communication
  - getting others to talk
  - tact
  - tolerance of other's mistakes
  - giving thanks and encouragement
  - keep everyone informed
  - using information technology

5 Motivating
  - inspiring others
  - providing realistic challenges
  - helping others to set goals and targets
  - helping others to value their own contributions and achievements

6 Evaluating
  - comparing outcomes with intentions
  - self-evaluation
  - evaluating the work of others
  - taking corrective action where necessary

One of the ways of creating an enhanced view of human potential in the management of change is to proceed on the basis of a wider view of personal aptitude and capability. An integrated, holistic and systemic view of intelligence helps to change the concept of management from one of channelling limited capability to one of realizing and empowering unlimited potential.

The brain

One of the problems with traditional education and particularly traditional methods of teaching is the understanding of the way the brain works. As educators we have radically misperceived the nature of the brain. During the last fifteen years or so research has discovered that the brain is infinitely more complex than we had ever assumed. One of the main discoveries is that we have two upper brains rather than one and that they operate in different ways with different purposes (see Table 2).

Traditional teaching methods have placed an almost obsessive emphasis on the functions that are located in the left hemisphere – giving greater attention to the memorizing of facts, the search for single correct answers and an attention to logical sequence. Research has also shown that where learners are encouraged to utilize a mental area, particularly those located

Table 2 Upper parts of the brain

Left hemisphere	Right hemisphere
language	rhythm
logic	music
number	images
sequence	imagination
linearity	daydreaming
analysis	colour

in the right hemisphere, this improves performance in other areas (Buzan 1982). In other words, where learners are encouraged to engage in the brain functions of imagery, imagination and rhythm in the pursuit of knowledge and understanding then learning is more successful. Two of the 'great brains' – Leonardo da Vinci and Albert Einstein – are examples of achievers who worked through an elegant synthesis of left and right brain activity. Clearly this has fundamental implications for the way in which we organize learning in formal educational settings. It gives added emphasis for the creation of both a liberally balanced curriculum and also broad and varied teaching methods. One of the most frequently raised criticisms of teachers in official reports and surveys by Her Majesty's Inspectors has been that of the underestimation of pupil abilities. A great deal of work needs to be done to build a clear and comprehensive insight into the nature and extent of human potential and how it can be released successfully in classrooms and workplaces.

Another crucial consideration is the fact that we have also hugely under-estimated the power of the brain and the capacity of the young to achieve far more than we have ever thought possible. This awesome potential also improves with age and the belief that mental activity declines as we get older is not supported by evidence. We know that if the brain is stimulated, no matter at what age it will continue to increase its capacity.

Motivation

For too long there has been a tendency to regard motivation as something managers do to workers to get better performance out of them. Reference has already been made to the pioneering work of Abraham Maslow who conceived the hierarchy of needs and the directional tendency towards self-actualization.

Attention to motivational factors is an important starting point for the selection of appropriate management styles. This process involves a sensitive understanding of staff needs and aspirations. These are likely to be complex and somewhat difficult to define explicitly. Each person involved in a work team or section is also likely to have a different pattern of needs and aspirations. Among the needs likely to be present in almost any group are the need to be:

- supported
- heard
- noticed
- encouraged
- trusted
- appreciated and valued
- informed
- helped to clarify ideas
- helped to develop skills and abilities
- challenged and extended

When the culture of the organization satisfies these particular needs people tend to work harder, with greater commitment and with a more purposeful sense of direction. Leadership can be said to be effective when staff consistently experience these motivational factors. Creating the culture which satisfies these needs is vital to the success of an organization and the quality of service it provides. Further insight is provided by Frederick Herzberg (1966) who has observed that in organizations workers are highly motivated when:

1 The work itself is intrinsically satisfying and challenging.
2 Workers have a decision making role and are involved in the co-management of the organization.
3 Successful work leads to recognition and the possibility of career advancement.

He also observed that workers are badly motivated when:

1 They are over-supervised and there are too many rules and regulations governing personal as well as professional activity.
2 Workers have difficult relationships with senior staff and when 'bossy' attitudes cause frustration and anxiety.
3 There are poor relationships with co-workers, low staff morale and divisive attitudes.
4 The working conditions are poor.

Herzberg undertook the research that led to these insights in the late 1950s, but only now are they beginning to be taken seriously as the paradigm shift gives them a fresh impetus.

Handy (1976) emphasizes the importance of acknowledging individual choice and decision making in motivation.

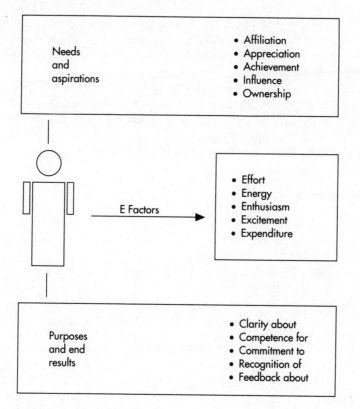

Figure 2   The motivation calculus

The 'E' factors shown in Figure 2 represent the amount of energy, effort, excitement and expenditure an individual decides to invest in any activity. The motivation calculus is the mechanism by which we decide how much 'E' to invest.

This model highlights a number of key elements that need to figure in management behaviour at the interpersonal level, and in the development of a culture supportive of human potential, endeavour and achievement:

1 The work that we do needs to respond to deep needs for satisfaction within ourselves.
2 The work we do needs to provide opportuntities to satisfy aspirations and achieve results.
3 Energy, effort, excitement and expenditure are decisions of individuals, not the inputs of managers or leaders.

Managers are in the business of helping to satisfy needs and this demands a sensitive attention to the thoughts and feelings of the staff involved. Effective managers are those who have a capacity to sense a pattern of needs in those they work with and to adapt their working style accordingly. Motivation is a key consideration in management and it is useful to be aware of three components: the needs to be satisfied; the aspirations to be achieved; self-esteem.

In managing, treating all people the same is a recipe for difficulty and disappointment. The guiding principle should be to treat people appropriately according to their perceived needs and aspirations and with a sensitivity to their self-esteem. This involves a careful combining of the professional, personal and managerial skills discussed earlier in this chapter.

Human potential

Organizations do not have a good track record of creating conditions of trust in which people are able to give of their best. Coercive and controlling styles of leadership and management do little to create commitment or to release locked up skills and abilities. Some understanding of the concept of human potential is important.

This concept suggests that living is a process of becoming – a gradual unfolding of personhood. Leading humanistic psychologists such as Abraham Maslow and Carl Rogers have argued that individuals have within themselves vast resources for healthy and successful living. These resources become minimalized and suppressed during the process of socialization but can be rekindled if a supportive psychological climate is created. Such an actualizing tendency is a characteristic of human beings but is also present in all organisms. Traditional styles of management have tended to reinforce the suppression of potential, and senior staff in organizations have tended not to concern themselves with building the psychological climate in which this directional tendency can be promoted. Leaders need to consider to what extent the current culture and climate of their organizations provides conditions for human growth and development, and the extent to which supposed under-performance can be attributed to the undernourishing quality of the human environment. Successful leadership is very much a process of activating potential and of providing the space and conditions in which it can be creatively expressed. A key aim for leaders is the cultivation of the actualizing tendency in themselves and in each and every member of staff. This emphasizes the processes of releasing and empowering, rather than those of controlling and supervising – for so long the prevailing behaviour of those in authority.

Self-concept

Two ideas very relevant to the process of change are that of psychological success (Argyris 1964) and the future focused role image (Singer 1974).

Psychological success is vital to the healthy survival and growth of a positive self-concept. It helps us to feel a strong sense of both competence and self-confidence in relation to those aspects of our lives in which we expend energy and effort. Change, particularly where externally imposed can pose threats to psychological success and consequently to the self-concept. Managers and leaders can reduce this threat, and support change in individuals by helping them to:

1 Understand the challenges involved in change and the nature of expected end results.
2 Formulate personal goals for the journey of change.
3 Determine their own methods for reaching those goals and producing the desired end results.
4 Assimilate and incorporate new elements into the self-concept.

This is a delicate process requiring skill and sensitivity.

In times of rapid change the difficulty of envisioning future role images can cause confusion and anxiety. One of the key characteristics of personal growth and development is the formation within our minds of an anticipated self – how we want to become, or what we need to be. This is often most noticeable in the formation of career aspiration – three years as head of department, then deputy headship and then headship in about ten years time. The trouble is that the world will be somewhat different when that career plan is fulfilled. How different the current educational reality is from that anticipated ten years ago by many recently appointed headteachers, and how many are now reflecting, having successfully achieved their aspirations – 'This is not what I came into headship for.'

In striving to support educational and organizational change it will be necessary to give increased attention to the issue of the future focused role image in order that long-term goals based on present realities do not become too fixed too early leading to disappointment and frustration when they cannot be realized as hoped. Managers and organizations will need to accept that professional development will have to place personal goals alongside professional ones to help in the creation of appropriate temporal orientation and a more integrated and holistic self-concept where there is a more healthy relationship between the personal and the professional.

Locus of control

A further insight into behaviour within organizations is offered by the concept of 'locus of control'. Rotter (1981) suggests that it is possible to distinguish two particular control dynamics. The first of these identifies those people who feel very much in charge of themselves and agents of their own destinies as 'internals' – their locus of control is within themselves. Those who feel

that they have very little control over what happens to them are referred
to as 'externals' – their locus of control is perceived as being external to
themselves. Evidence by Phares (1976) makes it very clear that those who
operate their lives with an 'internal' dynamic are better able to make choices
in their lives, take responsibility for their own actions and the consequences
of them and are better able to cope with failure and learn successfully from
it. In particular Phares discovered that 'internals':

1 have greater self-control
2 are better at retaining information
3 ask more questions of people; notice more of what is happening about
   them
4 are less coercive when given power
5 see other people as being responsible for themselves
6 prefer activities requiring skill than those involving chance
7 have higher academic achievements
8 are more likely to delay gratification
9 accept more responsibility for their own behaviour
10 have more realistic reactions to their own successes and failures
11 are less anxious
12 exhibit less pathological behaviour

The clear implication from research work in this area is that when people
accept responsibility for themselves and their own behaviour and recognize
their own power to affect and influence the way that circumstances develop,
they will be likely to work more creatively and cooperatively to the benefit
of both themselves and the organization as a whole. Within the school
setting there is a clear need to identify and cultivate an 'internal' dynamic
both within the classrooms of the school but also within the management
culture itself.

Empowerment

This is a concept closely related to the actualizing tendency referred to
above. It concerns the capacity of individuals to take increasing responsibility for the satisfying of their personal and professional needs. It differs
from motivation in that empowerment places emphasis on the individual
for creating his or her own conditions for growth, for defining challenges
and for setting goals and targets. Central to this concept are a number of
key assumptions and values (Hopson and Scally 1981). These include:

1 Each person is a unique individual, worthy of respect.
2 Individuals are responsible for their own actions and behaviour.
3 Individuals are responsible for their own feelings and emotions and for
   their responses to the behaviours of others.

4 New situations, however unwelcome, contain opportunities for new learning and growth.
5 Mistakes are learning experiences and are seen as outcomes rather than failures.
6 The seeds of our growth are within us. Only we ourselves can activate our potential for creativity and growth.
7 We can all do more than we are currently doing to become more than we currently are.
8 Awareness brings responsibility and responsibility creates the opportunity for choice.
9 Our own fear is the major limiter to our growth.
10 Growth and development never end. Self-empowerment is not an end to be achieved but a constant process of becoming.

Within organizations those who operate in a self-empowered way are characterized by:

1 An acceptance that change and development are the natural order of things and that change is to be welcomed rather than shunned and avoided.
2 Having skills to initiate change and the capacity to learn new skills and ideas.
3 Taking personal responsibility for actions and behaviour.
4 Making clear goals for themselves and developing action programmes to meet them.
5 Being action biased.
6 Frequently reviewing, assessing and evaluating their own progress and seeking feedback from others.
7 Being concerned to see others taking greater responsibility for their own lives.

In the effective organization many staff will be operating in self-empowering ways. Attempting to create a climate which is person centred, motivating and empowering is a vital challenge to those involved in educational management and leadership. The pursuit of such positive ideas is likely to avoid the situation described by Lieberman and Hardie (1981):

> There is a lot of pain in human systems that doesn't have to be there. There is a lot of hope, aliveness and joy ready to flower when members of the system can learn how to nourish these positive qualities.

Life cycles

An effective change agent is one who in the process of promoting and supporting professional change is able to recognize and understand the complex processes of personal adaptation that inevitably accompany it.

Table 3 Erikson's stages of human development

Infancy	0 – 2	trust v. mistrust
Early childhood	2 – 4	autonomy v. shame and doubt
Play age	5 – 7	initiative v. guilt
School age	6 – 12	industry v. inferiority
Adolescence	13 – 19	identity v. role confusion
Young adulthood	20 – 30	intimacy v. isolation
Maturity	30 – 60	generativity v. stagnation
Old age	60 plus	integrity v. despair

Some understanding of developmental psychology is very useful in making connections between the personal and the professional in the change process. Knowing how best to help someone in the professional domain requires an appreciation that individual and personal factors will also contribute to the stance that an individual assumes.

Change is a common and constant feature of our personal lives. The process of growth, development and aging attend everyone and our relationships continually develop and modify in the light of experience. During the course of an average lifetime a person passes through a number of phases and stages. The developmental psychologist Erik Erikson (1977) has identified eight of these, as shown in Table 3.

This scheme offers a series of critical periods in the human life cycle. Each phase presents the individual with crucial development work to undertake – represented in the scheme by a pair of alternative orientations or stances towards life, the self and other people. If the surrounding environment provides sufficient opportunity and support for the polarities to be resolved, individuals acquire psychological sturdiness and social competence as they develop. For most people the resources available for support are variable and there is a tendency to move into successive phases with 'unfinished business' from the previous stage. Thus individuals are unable to bring to the work of the new phases the full range of psychological attributes necessary. The struggle into young adulthood is especially hazardous and most reach it with a surface ability to cope and make their way in the world but their inner lives can be characterized by psychological uncertainty and emotional confusion. In difficult relationships and under organizational pressure these inadequacies can be exposed and coping behaviours can often be accompanied by feelings of guilt, anger, resentment and despair. Many people travel through life deeply disappointed with the quality of their lives and their seeming incapacity to find effective and lasting strategies to life's difficulties and challenges.

Those involved in work as agents of change need to appreciate that the personal lives of individuals are characterized by a struggle to survive and find fulfilment. The ways that individuals behave in organizations, react to change and new expectations may be determined as much by the development struggles described by Erikson as by the particular details of the organizational issues at stake. A curiosity about human behaviour and a sensitivity to the psychological struggles of human living are an important part of being an effective manager and leader; they are also a vital attribute in undertaking consultancy work to assist the processes of change in organizations. This is not to say that those involved in management need to be analytical psychologists, but rather that they understand that most human behaviour is purposeful, serving powerful inner needs and aspirations.

In his analysis of teacher development, Leithwood (1990) has identified the following career cycle:

1 Launching the career.
2 Stabilizing: developing mature commitment feeling at ease, seeking more responsibility.
3 New challenges and concerns: diversifying, seeking added responsibilities.
4 Reaching a professional plateau: re-appraisal, sense of mortality, ceasing striving for promotion or stagnating and becoming cynical.
5 Preparing for retirement: focusing, disenchantment, serenity.

Bolam (1990) identifies five job stages:

1 Preparatory stage: When wishing to apply for a new job
2 Appointment stage: When selected or rejected
3 Induction stage: First two years in post
4 In-service stage: 3–5, 6–10, 11+ years in post
5 Transitional stage: Promotion, redeployment

Most organizations, even quite small ones are likely to contain people at different stages of these cycles. Clearly, the relationship to change will depend upon where in this cycle particular individuals have reached. A probationary teacher will want to establish some basic classroom stability and confidence before having to face a significant change in methodology. Teachers in mid-career, with promotion aspirations to the fore, may well look upon change as an opportunity to demonstrate improved competence and gain leadership experience. A deputy head in professional plateau, having decided against further promotion may look upon an early retirement as preferable to managing major change. Such factors relate strongly to motivation and will affect the 'E' factors referred to earlier. Too often the issue of life and career patterns in a staff is not something that is easily brought into general staff discussion, yet a common acceptance of patterns of professional diversity is essential if change objectives are to be met and the change process is to be managed appropriately and as comfortably as possible.

Life and career cycles are essential cultural issues that need to be acknowledged and responded to. The links between the personal and the professional will be blurred and they are not easily separated. Only by making our needs and aspirations clear and explicit can we create the pool of information from which sensible and appropriate decisions can be made and in order for managers and leaders to build a sensitive awareness of developmental needs and differences.

4

The dynamics of change

The learning process

Change involves moving from a present state to a different future one. Many changes, at both personal and organizational level, require new knowledge and skills to enable us to adapt successfully to new requirements and circumstances. Rites of passage are changes in the progress of our lives and these attract significant attention and celebration. At the age of eighteen we enter a world in which the framework of rights and responsibilities is restructured and the state acknowledges that we are now legally the agents of our own actions. The reality of this will depend upon locus of control and our capacity for leading a self-empowering life. In recognition of the range of changes that accompany entry into married life, a period of preparation or engagement has become an important social convention. During this time partners can prepare themselves so as to enter responsibly into a new style of relationship and a new way of living. During these times a great deal of learning takes place and a great deal of advice is offered. Yet it is sad that the learning process is regarded as the least significant we bring to the phase of preparation.

Learning has come to be associated with schooling – something which is done to you by others, as a state requirement. Much of it is structured on competition, success or failure and ratified by certification. The content of learning is set as the main objective – what we know. Very rarely does the schooling system help to develop in us a love of learning that will be lifelong, nor equip us with the skills to approach the significant journey of change in our lives as a series of significant learning challenges. Learning as exemplified by schooling is something that most of us want to leave behind.

Strongly associated with the concept of learning is dependence on the teacher, and many of us come to believe that learning inevitably requires the controlling presence of a teacher or instructor. Our obsession with teaching and instruction has stolen from the individual the awareness that one of our most significant genetic features is an awesome capacity for self-development, intellectual growth and self-directed learning. Natural learning, as Papert has observed, requires neither teacher nor curriculum and by the time most children start school they have exercised their huge learning potential in myriad ways to become sturdy individuals with skills of adaptation, self-management and communication well established. Research into the very early stages of life increasingly confirms the huge potential for self directed learning, active in the survival instincts of the newly born child.

John Holt has documented this well:

> Almost every child, on the first day he sets foot in a school building, is smarter, more curious, less afraid of what he doesn't know, better at finding and figuring things out, more confident, resourceful, persistent and independent, than he will ever again be in his schooling or, unless he is very unusual and lucky, for the rest of his life.
>
> (Holt 1971)

Describing entry into the classroom he says:

> In he comes, this curious, patient, determined, energetic, skilful learner. We sit him down at a desk, and what do we teach him? Many things. First, that learning is separate from living. 'You come to school to learn,' we say, as if the child hadn't been learning before, as if living were out there and learning were in here and there were no connection between the two. Secondly he cannot be trusted to learn and is no good at it. Everything we do about reading, a task far simpler than what the child has already mastered, says to him, 'If we don't make you read, you won't, and if you don't do it exactly the way we tell you, you can't.' In short, the child comes to feel that learning is a passive process, something that someone else does to you, instead of something you do for yourself.

Learning is central to the change process, it has attended all the most significant developments in our lives and enabled us to pursue our goals, make choices and generally make our way in the world. Yet even in institutions devoted to learning, this vital attribute is ignored or not regarded sufficient recognition. Professional development is essentially about professional learning, therefore we need to be aware that organizations which develop and adapt are by necessity learning organizations – concerned with gaining new knowledge, acquiring new skills and forging new values and beliefs. In short, learning is the essence of change and its prime requisite.

A central function of management and leadership is the facilitation of learning and the creating of a culture which is learning focused, curious about what it does not know, experimental in its development and rarely fearful of its mistakes.

Conditions for change

If we are to establish effective conditions for change we need to be aware of the conditions that encourage effective learning. One of the mostly damaging aspects of the learning process is the inculcation of the belief that individual failing in the schooling system is a dysfunction of the individual learner. It is a tragedy that given such awesome potential for growth and development so many young people in the first stage of their life's journey are made to feel 'failures'.

One of the major challenges for schools and colleges in the future is to reverse this situation and facilitate the paradigm shift described in Chapter 2. Toffler emphasizes the need to concentrate on developing the skills of self-directed learning:

> Given further acceleration, we can conclude that knowledge will grow increasingly perishable. Today's 'fact' becomes tomorrow's misinformation. This is no argument against learning facts or data – far from it. But a society in which the individual constantly changes his job, place of residence, his social ties and so forth places an enormous premium on learning efficiency. Tomorrow's schools must therefore teach not merely data, but ways to manipulate it. Students must learn how to discard old ideas, how and when to replace them. They must, in short, learn how to learn.
>
> (Toffler 1971)

Our incapacities in this area can cause a shocked paralysis when major change confronts us – we do not know what to do, how to gain more information, how to envision a different future, to plan a course of action. Change is experienced as a threat rather than an opportunity, as something to be avoided if possible rather than something to be welcomed.

Perhaps it is a deep seated fear of 'getting it wrong', of being found deficient that terrifies us. For many of us there is still the lingering but powerful association between learning and punishment. Nowhere is this more graphically illustrated than in the child-rearing manuals studied by Alice Miller in *For Your Own Good*:

> In school, discipline precedes the actual teaching. There is no sounder pedagogical axiom than the one that children must first be trained

before they can be taught. There can be discipline without instruction, but no instruction without discipline.
We insist therefore that learning in and of itself is not discipline, is not moral endeavour, but discipline is an essential part of learning.
The perverse will, which to its own and other's detriment is not in command of itself, must be broken.

(Miller 1987a)

No wonder we have to struggle so hard in the schools of the late twentieth century to achieve a more liberating and enriching learning process for the students. It is only very recently, and somewhat reluctantly, that corporal punishment has been withdrawn as an agent of control in the learning process of schools.

In creating conducive conditions for change we must do whatever we can to erase fear, to remove the anxiety about mistakes and getting things wrong. These are organizational toxins that will continue to stifle creativity and development as long as they are allowed to flourish in the hearts and minds of any of us.

In their studies of successful companies, Peters and Waterman point to the recognition among leading managers that failure is inevitable:

If I wasn't making mistakes, I wasn't making decisions.
You cannot innovate unless you are willing to accept mistakes.

(Peters and Waterman 1982)

In management terms it is not only an expectation that mistakes will be made, but an acceptance of them as a desirable and necessary target. In *Thriving on Chaos* (1988), Peters has this advice:

The goal is to be more than tolerant of slip ups. You must . . . actively encourage failure. Talk it up. Laugh about it. Go round the table at a project group or staff meeting. Start with your own most interesting foul up. Then have everyone follow suit. What mistakes did you make this week? What were the most interesting ones? How can we help you make more mistakes, faster?

He also points out that people who do not make enough mistakes are not taking enough chances.

Reflective practice

One of the ways that we can begin to break down the dependency of the learner on the teacher and develop self-directed learning is by taking note of significant breakthroughs that have taken place in the area of adult learning over the past twenty years.

Adult and professional learning

A vital source of help and information is contained in the set of ideas, principles and theories that together constitute Adult Education. This field of education has seen enormous developments in both theory and practice in recent years and those involved in managing professional development and training, both within schools and outside them, would benefit from its ideas and practices. In particular the following ten principles for adult learning will provide a useful starting point:

1 voluntary participation
2 mutual respect
3 collaboration
4 action and reflection
5 organizational setting
6 choice and change
7 social, economic and cultural factors
8 motivation
9 critical thinking
10 self-direction

The implications of these principles are:

1 Teachers are voluntary participants in professional development, they engage in it as a result of personal choice.
2 A relationship of mutual respect needs to be established between participants and tutors if the optimum conditions for effective learning are to be established. It is also essential for tutors to recognize that they too are learners, capable of learning from the different experiences of course members.
3 Adult learning is a collaborative experience and needs to be viewed by tutors as a relationship of equals.
4 A vital feature of adult learning is the process of action and reflection – looking back on past experience in order to make decisions about the future.
5 INSET tutors need to remember that most professional activity in education takes place in an organizational setting. This adds complexities and special challenges to the process of change.
6 In adults, personal and professional change can be difficult and painful. As a result of previous experience some adults find it very hard to accept help and guidance. Trying to change their ways of working can involve loss of confidence and self-esteem.
7 Differences in the social, economic and cultural backgrounds of course attenders need to be respected and taken account of in designing and developing INSET activities.
8 The motivation to learn is a key consideration. Professional adults bring

a wide variety of needs, hopes and aspirations to their own professional development.

9 One of the most important contributions a tutor can make to this learning partnership is to promote and facilitate a climate of critical thinking in which course members are encouraged to lay open to examination their professional thinking and practice.

10 A key aim of those involved in adult learning is to encourage self-direction. This involves gradually reducing dependence on the tutor and supporting the learner's own aspirations, learning strategies and self-evaluation.

Reflective practice

Those involved in designing and facilitating the professional development of their colleagues need to encourage what Donald Schön has called 'reflective practitioners'. These are teachers who value the opportunity to explore their practical professionalism in structured situations, whether by their own self-directed process of critical reflection or in the more formal setting of an in-service course. This process is illustrated in Figure 3.

Critical reflection is a process whereby we submit to examination incidents and events in our past in order to make sense of them and place them within our system of professional ideas and values. We also reflect on past experience in order to sort out what we consider to be specific successes and difficulties. With the detailed information that we are able to derive from this process we are in a good position to look ahead to the future incidents and events on our professional calendar, to make precise practical plans in the light of what we have learnt. This iterative process of action, reflection and planning is at the heart of all professional learning and it is what we need to structure skilfully in the professional development activities we design and facilitate.

Closely related to Schön's concept is the process referred to as experiential learning. Developed by David Kolb (1984) and others, this approach

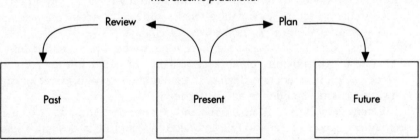

Figure 3 The reflective practitioner

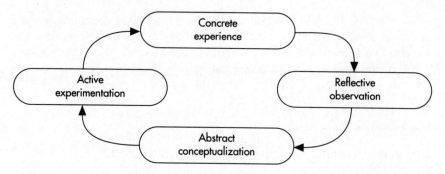

Figure 4 Experiential learning cycle

suggests a cycle of discrete mental processes following concrete experience, as illustrated in Figure 4.

In order to make sense of experience it is necessary to reflect and think about it. This enables the experience to be assimilated into an individual's framework of concepts and constructs. Further thinking may follow in which new learning is used to formulate new concepts and build new constructs which can be acted upon.

One of the disadvantages of the cyclic model is that it constantly turns in upon itself whereas the cycle repeats itself with new material each time new experience is encountered. A modified version of the model, shown in Figure 5, illustrates this.

Using this model as a basis for designing programmes of professional development enables many of the adult learning principles listed earlier to

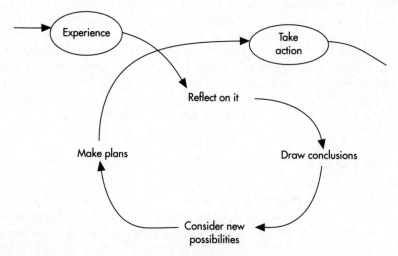

Figure 5 Developmental learning cycle

be respected and acknowledged. It is important to remember that the most precious resource teachers bring with them to training is their experience. A course or workshop creates a 'time out' opportunity to use the process of critical reflection both to make sense of past experience and also of the learning experiences structured within the workshop itself.

Learning from experience

A great deal has been written about learning from experience. It is important to make a distinction between:

1 Incidental learning from experience
2 Deliberate and planned learning from experience

The first is essentially a casual process where we think about experiences, rehearse preferred alternatives in our minds and generally imagine what might have happened if things had been different. Deliberate learning from experience is altogether more focused and purposeful. It involves the submitting of particular experiences to systematic review in order to learn from them and so improve in the future. In this way learning from experience becomes a conscious process of reflection and improvement.

In the light of earlier comments about 'failure' and mistakes, it is significant that the phrase 'trial and error' has a more general acceptability in our social vocabulary than 'trial and success'. When we catalogue our achievements and work out which behaviours were responsible we increase awareness of our strengths and qualities and create opportunities for building on them in the future.

The successful change organization is one in which experience is regarded as a key resource for learning and development. This involves a great deal of open debate and discussion about what goes on, what seems to be working well, where the snags are occurring and what each participant is learning moment by moment and day by day. The question 'How are we doing?' is endlessly addressed. There is a passion for information and a yearning for insight and understanding. No stone can remain unturned in the search for excellence and in the pursuit of quality.

Purpose and focus

In cultivating a learning organization attuned to change and development, it is essential to acknowledge the two levels of learning activity: pupils and students; teachers and managers. A significant part of the paradigm shift in education is the idea that it is within the second group that there is the greater need for learning.

In *The Learning Organization*, Bob Garratt (1987) raises the idea of organizational ecology – people in relationship to each other and to the organizational environment in which they work – and uses the formula developed by Revens (1982):

$$L \geqslant C$$

This suggests that for an organization to develop, change and survive successfully, its rate of learning L must be equal to, or greater than, the rate of change C in the external environment. The recent experience in education would seem to suggest that a different formula has been at work:

$$C \geqslant L$$

Change has been coming at schools at a perilously faster rate than their capacity to 'tool up' for new systems and procedures. Since it is unlikely that we can affect the pace of change, which will probably accelerate, then survival can only be guaranteed by increasing the organizational capacity to learn and adapt.

One way to do this is to try to extract some basic principles upon which healthy organizational learning can be built. A useful start can be made by giving attention to two specific aspects of the learning process: the purposes for learning, and the focus of the learning.

Define the purpose

Designing effective programmes of professional learning and development depends very much on achieving a successful match between the skills and abilities of the provider and the needs and expectations of the participants. Establishing clear purposes can help to do this. Table 4 suggests ten different purposes.

Table 4   Purposes for professional learning

INFORM	the need to KNOW
FAMILIARIZE	the need to UNDERSTAND
ADAPT	the need to CHANGE
DEVELOP	the need to EXTEND
IMPLEMENT	the need to INNOVATE
ENCOURAGE	the need to BUILD CONFIDENCE
TRAIN	the need to ACQUIRE NEW SKILLS
REFLECT	the need to MAKE SENSE OF EXPERIENCE
EXPLORE	the need to CONSIDER POSSIBILITIES
REVIEW	the need to ASSESS AND EVALUATE

While most programmes of professional development will have more than one purpose, this list does help to recognize the range of needs that are required to be catered for in planning. It is important to establish early in the planning process which particular purposes are being served, since different needs will require different treatment. Establishing purposes is an essential first step in planning. Table 4 offers a useful checklist of purposes to help ascertain the precise needs that are being pursued.

Establish the focus

Practical competence in teaching is essentially about the relationship of skill to knowledge and most professional development is focused on one or other of these. What this model attempts to show is the vital importance of the 'P' factor – those unique elements of our own personality which make us what we are (see Figure 6).

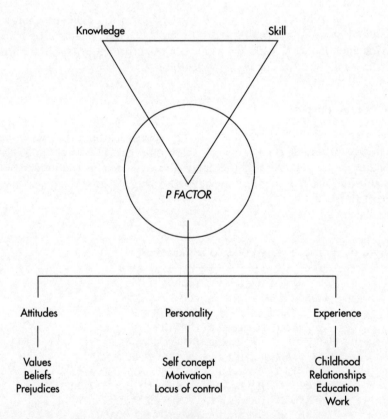

Figure 6 Focus for professional learning and development

1   Attitudes

Our response to any planned programme of professional development will
be affected by the unique set of values, attitudes and beliefs that we have
accumulated in our lifetimes to date. While we will share many of these
with others, no one else has exactly the same set. Our attitudinal stance is
also in a state of change: it is rarely fixed and modifies in the light of new
experience. New experiences can also tend to confirm or contradict particular prejudices we have developed. These prejudices are particularly strong
beliefs based on generalised understanding and tend to arouse our feelings
and emotions.

2   Personality

The self-concept refers to our own view of ourselves. We might be confident and optimistic about ourselves at particular times but in certain
situations feel frustrated and unable to cope well. The decisions and choices
we make in our lives are crucially affected by this self-understanding.

Motivation refers to the internal drives and forces that incline us towards
particular behaviours. They may be connected with the striving to satisfy
needs, to achieve aspirations or to conform to our view of ourselves – the
self-concept – and how we think we should be in different situations.

Locus of control refers in general terms to a tendency either to see our
lives as being controlled from outside ourselves – by parents, partners,
bosses or the state; or from within ourselves – controlled by our own decisions and choices.

Each of these factors relate powerfully to the sort of teacher and organization member we become and will affect our capacity to respond in particular ways when faced with the need to learn, during school based
professional development activities or at INSET events.

3   Experience

All the factors that have contributed to the pattern of experiences that have
made us what we are – our childhood, our education, our relationships and
our work situations – will have a bearing on our capacity to learn and
change.

Each of these FOCUS points relate to our work as managers of change.
The 'P' factor must never be ignored – it affects all that we do – whether
it be acquiring a new skill or taking on new information. In structuring
professional development activities we need to offer opportunities for professional learners to relate new skills or knowledge to their experience in
a climate of psychological safety and critical thinking. It will help us to see

our professional colleagues as 'reflective practitioners' and providing opportunities for them to exercise the 'P' factor in their continued learning and
daily work.

Both purpose and focus need to be at the forefront of our minds as we
undertake the process of planning and preparation for programmes of
change. They should be the central point of discussions when we are re-
quested to provide some specific professional development activities and
also at the centre of our thinking when it comes to the planning of the
change itself.

Dimensions of learning and development

Professional development involves the expanding of our ability to produce
the results we truly want in our work. It is useful to consider the dynamic
relationship between three key dimensions of the learning process, as illustrated in Figure 7.

Our professional practice – what we say and do in pursuit of organizational aims and purposes – is informed by what we think and how we
feel. This dynamic relationship determines the nature of our professional

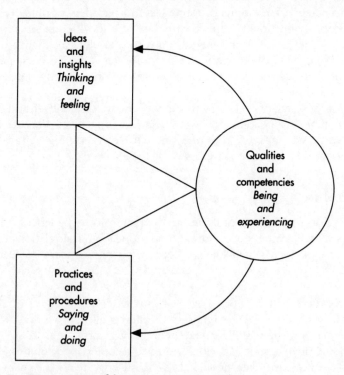

Figure 7   Dimensions of learning

qualities and competencies – how we are and what we experience as participants in the organizational drama. As we reflect on our actions we create new ideas and insights which further inform what we will say or do differently, or the same, in the future. Learning is systematic – relating to the vibrant interaction of thinking, feeling, intuition and physical action.

This model provides a useful framework for assessing and reflecting on our professional work and the extent to which we employ a deliberate rather than an incidental approach to learning and development. If we want to extend our qualities and competencies we need to take account of our mental models, our thinking structures and our ways of managing emotions and feelings. In addition, we need to consider to what extent our practices and our procedures are dependent upon fixed patterns of thinking and feeling.

In their study of the ways that different organizations respond to pressures exerted by the external environment, Miles and Snow (1978) generated three distinct types of behaviour:

1 'Defender' organizations that strive for stability by discouraging competition.
2 'Analyser' organizations that are alert to new possibilities but only if viability can be established.
3 'Prospector' organizations which respond well to turbulence and uncertainty, striving to find new opportunities by sustaining an 'innovation edge'.

These styles can also be applied to professional learning. Defender learning is about clinging on to what has always been known and avoiding situations which require new ideas, skills or competencies. Analyser learning accepts that some new knowledge and skill may be necessary but only if there is no alternative. Prospector learning begins with the assumption that progress into the future can only be sustained on the basis of continuous, systematic learning. It is this approach which is at the heart of the learning organization.

Resistance to change

Given the inhibiting influences of our upbringing and education we should not be surprised that we have developed considerable aptitude in resisting change in its various forms and guises. As managers we should realize that resisting change is very purposeful behaviour – it is a strategy to protect ourselves in the face of threats to self-esteem and psychological survival.

The notion of the future focused role image has already been referred to. We invest a great deal of physical, intellectual, emotional and psychological energy in constructing our role images and comfortably occupying the organizational niches we have created for ourselves. When change is proposed, or enforced, then the role image upon which we have based our behaviour is declared null and void and we have, as yet, no alternative with which to replace it. We may feel bereft of the psychological props upon which much of our personal and professional credibility is built. So we fight to remain intact by seeking to preserve the status quo, or as much of it as we possibly can. One of the ways of doing this is to attack the proposition and find as much fault as possible with what is intended:

- We tried that once before and it didn't work
- We don't have the time
- Let's get back to reality
- We don't have the resources
- You can't teach an old dog new tricks
- Not that again!
- We've managed so far without it
- Let's form a working party
- It won't work in our department
- Let's wait until things settle down
- We've always done it this way and no one has complained

These phrases will have a familiar ring to them and some we will identify as part of our own resistance strategy during some events in our lives. They echo something of the defender and analyser positions described above.

Away from the personal level, a range of reasons for organizational resistance to change is offered by Roger Plant (1987):

- fear of the unknown
- lack of information
- misinformation
- historical factors
- threat to core skills and competence
- threat to status
- threat to power base
- no perceived benefits
- low trust organizational culture
- poor relationships
- fear of failure
- fear of looking stupid
- reluctance to experiment
- custom bound
- reluctance to let go
- strong peer group norms

He goes on to suggest that resistance to change comes in two forms – systemic and behavioural. Systemic resistance tends to occur when there is a lack of knowledge, information, skill and managerial capacity. It is almost as if the organization is crying out – 'We can't do this!' Behavioural resistance is more emotionally centred and derives from the reactions, perceptions and assumptions of individuals and groups in the organization. Lack of trust, for example, is much more difficult to manage than lack of information or the absence of resources.

The resistance voltage will be greater, Plant suggests, if levels of involvement and information are low:

> The less I know about plans to change, the more I assume, the more suspicious I become, and the more I direct my energy into counterproductive 'resister games'. Once I feel manipulated, or uninvolved, I will inevitably tend to veer towards a negative view of the change and its effect on me.

The challenges for managers and leaders are often compounded by paranoia – the resistance is directed at them personally. Coulson (1985) has provided a valuable insight into the psychology of change which offers guidance to managers as they contemplate the way forward in their schools and colleges. This can be summarized as four points:

1 Initiators of the management of change need to be aware that when change is suggested, those involved in it tend to want to protect what they see themselves to be.
2 The way that individuals operate in their particular work situations has come about through a long process of establishing an identity in relation to the demands and expectations raised. They strive to satisfy their own work needs and the expectations of others with the minimum of uncertainty and anxiety. Pressure to alter this way of being tend to be received as threats to the comfortable continuity of living and working.
3 Suggestions that they change their way of doing things and their approaches to the professional tasks for which they have responsibility imply a level of inadequacy in their performance and this threatens the identity they have striven to develop. The natural inclination is to become aroused in the defence of the familiar and established.
4 Far too often headteachers and senior staff experience this defensive tendency as opposition to new ideas and see their task as one of overcoming the perceived resistance. A battle of wills can ensue which is counter-productive to the developments themselves and to the professional relationships which are so vital to their success.

Much of this polarization can be avoided if the following six factors are remembered:

1 When people resist change they are not usually working in active opposition to it as such, but demonstrating that a threat to their personal and professional security has been experienced.

2 Senior managers need to accept this response as natural and inevitable.
3 A key task for managers and leaders is to listen to the experience of those
  involved in change and seek to understand what is felt to be threatened.
4 Managers need to be deeply caring and concerned about what it is that
  staff feel they are having to give up and to be seen as an ally in this
  process, and not as an opponent.
5 Managers also need to help colleagues to protect what they perceive to
  be under threat while moving them towards new methods and strategies.
6 In the process of change it is vital to try to avoid undermining the individual's sense of competence and professional well-being by appearing
  to reject or devalue their established practices.

Much pain and discomfort can be avoided if some of these key ideas are
incorporated in the values and assumptions which underpin approaches to
management and leadership. A great deal of stress within school staffs can
be traced back to insensitive and clumsy handling of innovation and change.

Phases in changing

For the individuals involved, change will involve moving from the familiar
to the unfamiliar, from the known to the unknown. A key management role
is to assist this process. It is important to be aware of the effects change can
have, particularly when it is imposed. A very useful insight into this process
has been provided by Steve Fink. He suggests that any substantial change
in our lives involves a sequence of reactive stages: *Shock, withdrawal,
acknowledgement* and *adaptation.*

Shock

The shock stage can involve strong emotional feelings of confusion and
disbelief, a sense that the familiar structures and boundaries of the world
are crumbling. A familiar feeling is – 'this cannot be happening to me'. Clear
and coherent thought is difficult to apply in the face of strong feelings and
sometimes wild and irrational solutions are a characteristic verbal response.
Organizational changes are seldom as traumatic as bereavement, accident
or a relationship crisis, but when threatened or imposed from outside or
above can involve a sense of disorientation, confusion and threat.

Withdrawal

Withdrawal follows when awareness of the implications of the changes
begin to emerge. In an attempt to keep the familiar world intact, people
search for ways of avoiding the consequences of change and struggle to

maintain the status quo. At this stage, counter-arguments will be rehearsed and resistance rationales developed. Time alone with our thoughts is important as we struggle to come to terms with new demands and requirements.

Acknowledgement

Eventually a sense of the inevitability of the changes will begin to emerge. There is a realization that energy to resist avoidance will need to be greater than that required to go forward with the flow of new developments. There is also a need to keep in step and not to draw too much attention to behaviour. A fear of isolation, of perhaps being deserted by others, particularly from those we look to for approval is also very strong. Acknowledgement is often accompanied by a deep sense of uncertainty and insecurity. While it may be necessary to accept the seemingly inevitable it is not always clear that the resources to move from the known to the unknown will be sufficient for change to be achieved without difficulty, discomfort and loss.

Adaptation

Adaptation is reached when rational acceptance of change is matched by emotional and psychological adjustment. Inner confusion and uncertainty begin to give way as preparations for change are made, anxieties are reduced and the practical steps forward identified. Adaptation involves an internal switch from attachment to the ways of the past to a belief that the future will at least be all right and at best beneficial and rewarding. Adaptation does not necessarily require conformity. It can involve compromise and sometimes a determination to pursue passive resistance. For perhaps a few, adaptation will involve a departure from the situation altogether and the pursuit of another job.

There is nothing systematic or predictable about this model. In some circumstances we can move through the phases in a matter of minutes, in other more traumatic situations the stages can take years to work through and may never be fully resolved. For those involved in the management, promotion and support of change the theory is useful for a number of reasons:

1 It can help to understand the nature of individual behaviour.
2 It can provide a basis for working with groups and individuals in identifying appropriate support strategies and interventions.
3 It offers a scheme for planning change and development projects.

An important factor to bear in mind is that while as individuals we move through these stages, we do so at different rates and in different ways. The management of change can frequently seem to be so complex and

challenging because at any one time individual members of the organization can be at different stages of the model. Some enthusiasts, anxious for
change can be adapting while others are transfixed in shock. Withdrawers
will be resisting for all they are worth while acknowledgers can be raising
questions, airing anxieties and seeking reassurance.

It is essential to have strategies to deal with the needs created at each of
these four stages. These can be summarised as follows.

Managing the shock stage

The key stance is conveying an acceptance of the effects that change can
have on people. Strategies will need to include:

• acknowledging and accepting the state of shock
• offering understanding
• conveying empathy
• creating opportunities for perceived grievances to be aired
• encouraging the disclosure of feelings

Managing the withdrawal stage

The key stance is accepting that resistance to change is a natural reaction.
Strategies will need to include:

• a counselling approach which encourages individuals to disclose their
  frustrations and anxieties
• providing sensitive and attentive listening
• sensing the anxieties involved

Managing the acknowledgement stage

The key stance is that of being ready and able to provide information and
explanation. Strategies will include

• helping others to activate their resources for change by reviewing appropriate skills and competency

While it is useful to rehearse the arguments against change it is important
not to be too reassuring or to engage in 'don't worry' tactics. Adaptation will
follow as and when individuals develop a sense of their own innate capacity for change.

Managing the adaptation stage

The key stance is that of providing practical help and support. Strategies
will include:

- designing new systems and procedures
- developing familiarity with new resources and materials
- considering new methods and techniques
- being available with practical help

Zones of uncertainty

What these statements conceal is the considerable confusion, anger and uncertainty that change often stirs up inside organizations. A further insight into the process of change and the individual is supplied by the concept of 'zones of uncertainty'. This phrase, coined by Donald Schön (1971) suggests that change involves risks in moving from the familiar to the unfamiliar.

As Figure 8 suggests the first step out of the comfort of the familiar can be the most hazardous, involving a range of risks and difficulties. It is important to be sensitive to three particular clusters of feelings:

1 Loss
- of firmly held beliefs and ideas
- of established patterns of behaviours
- of comfortable habits
- of confidence and self-esteem

2 Anxiety
- about required levels of understanding
- about new skills
- about what the future will be like
- about being able to cope
- about being seen as different

3 Struggle
- to survive intact
- to acquire new competence
- to gain respect and recognition

Among the most valuable of managerial qualities are those that convey an informed and sensitive understanding of the impact of change and of the difficulties that have to be faced to accomplish it.

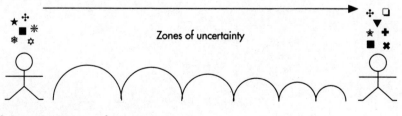

Figure 8 Zones of uncertainty

But change must never be regarded as something that has to be feared, resisted and avoided. Change can present us with new opportunities and exciting prospects. It can focus our thinking and concentrate our ambitions. It is through change that we will realize our wilder dreams.

While it is vital to be sensitive to apparent difficulties it is also important to recognize the powerful range of human resources that can be activated within each person. As we know, people will tend to under-perform if expectations of them are too low. Within organizations, people will inhibit the full expression of their skills and abilities if they feel oppressed and underestimated. Over recent years organizational development theory has placed increasing emphasis on the importance of assumptions about workers and their work. Successful managers have been found to be those who are able to activate the inner resources of their colleagues by building a positive and enhanced climate of assumptions.

The learning organization

In the face of rapid and accelerating change it is increasingly necessary to see learning in the organizational context as well as at the individual level. The phrase 'the learning organization' is a strongly emerging concept. Garratt (1987) argues that learning has become the key development commodity of an organization:

> Generating and selling know-how and know-why, the learning of the organization and its people, is becoming the core of any organization

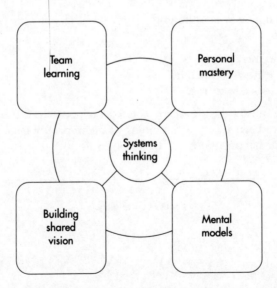

Figure 9 Five core disciplines for developing learning organization

which has the chance of surviving in the longer term. We already know a lot about organizational learning processes. When this is added to the new ideas on the generation of vision, the refinement of thinking processes, the development of policy and strategy, the notion of managing as a 'holistic' process, and the acquisition of new managerial skills from outside the traditional boundaries, then there is a powerful mix available.

It is to such a powerful mix that Peter Senge attends in his book about the learning organization. In *The Fifth Discipline* (1990) he suggests that learning organizations are the ones which have destroyed the illusion that the world is created of separated and unrelated forces. He proposes a set of five learning disciplines which will converge to create powerful and effective organizations of change (see Figure 9).

Systems thinking

This is the overarching discipline. It is the discipline for seeing wholes, patterns and relationships of change. It looks for the structures that underlie complex situations and involves a shift of mind and thinking (see Table 5).

Systems thinking involves all participants in an organization sharing responsibility for the problems generated by a system and for developing the creative solutions to them.

Table 5 Systems thinking

From	To
Seeing parts	Seeing wholes
Seeing people as helpless reactors in reality	Seeing people as active participants in shaping their reality
Reacting to the present	Creating the future

Personal mastery

The learning organization will be one that transcends the traditional organizational assumptions about human potential and which recognizes that people are the active force in the pursuit of organizational aims, with a wealth of energy, skill and talent available for realising them.

A key characteristic of the learning organization is the recognition by leaders of the 'sacredness of their responsibility' for the lives of their people.

Supporting each participant to strive for personal mastery involves helping them to approach their working life from a creative rather than a restrictive viewpoint. It embodies the process of continual clarification of what is important and learning how to see current reality more clearly, recognizing that current reality is an ally and not an enemy.

Personal mastery stems from a dynamic relationship between vision – a clear picture of a desired future, and purpose – a specific driving force towards it. This can create structural conflicts between the tensions drawing individuals towards their goals and the tensions anchoring them to traditional beliefs and values. The learning organization creates a relentless willingness to root out the ways in which we limit or deceive ourselves from seeing what really is.

Mental models

The future, Senge suggests, will require us to abandon our reliance on linear and vertical thinking as the chief sources of mental activity. Creativity and the greater use of imagination and intuition will need to balance the preoccupation with rationality and logic. Increasing reliance will need to be placed on the use of reflection and enquiry skills, particularly those that enable us to challenge the assumptions that hinder and inhibit the building of creative scenarios for change. Far from being private and personal possessions our mental models will need to be more open to enquiry and comment from our colleagues so that we can avoid what Argyris calls 'skilled incompetence' – that capacity to protect ourselves from the pain and threat posed by new learning situations.

Building shared vision

The learning organization is one that engages in the active process of envisioning – a collaborative activity to design and describe the future that reflects the collective aims and aspirations of those making up the organization. In this sense vision needs to be seen as a calling rather than simply a good idea. Shared vision can uplift people's aspirations, create sparks of excitement, compel experimentation and risk taking and increase the courage to succeed. Shared vision can never be 'official', it needs both to bubble up the organization as well as to filter down, connecting personal visions in an elaborate tracery of ambition and purpose. Vision is not to be seen as a solution to problems, but rather a driving force for the process of co-creation. It is the central element of the leader's work, relentless and never ending. It involves constant attention to three key questions:

1 What does the future we are seeking to create look like?
2 Why are we pursuing this particular vision?
3 How do we behave to be consistent with the vision we have created?

Team learning

Learning organizations have recognized for some time that collaboration together with a proper individualism is the key source of dynamic strength for development. An increasing tendency to tackle work through task groups and temporary teams requires attention to the processes of collaboration as well as to the work itself. This requires a focus on collective learning if the potential of participants is to be harnessed effectively. There will need to be an enhanced capacity to use conflict creatively, to use dialogue rather than discussion to root out defective thinking habits and defensive routines. The process of action learning defined by Revens (1962) involving team members using the experience of the work itself as the chief source for improvement will need to become a way of life.

These five learning disciplines, Senge argues, will converge to create powerful and effective learning organizations. While developing separately, each will prove critical to the other's success, just as in any effective ensemble. Each provides a vital dimension in building organizations that can truly learn and enhance their capacity to realize their highest aspirations. Success and achievement will depend upon certain characteristics being developed:

1 A shift from an instrumental to a sacred attitude to work.
2 A community where mutual support replaces individual exploitation.
3 A covenant between the individual and the organization as opposed to a contract.

The learning organization is one that is geared to change and determined to develop and refine its capacities to move into the future with confidence, curiosity and commitment.

5

Leadership and change

Terms and definitions

One of the great challenges to a new paradigm in organizational development is the redefinition of the terms leadership and management. Our education and upbringing, and indeed our daily engagement with national and international news tend to equate leadership with leaders – those in powerful positions in international and institutional affairs. For those concerned to help in the development of effective leadership this has tended to create problems of definition. We have a tendency to think of leadership in terms of role and personality – that leadership can only be considered as a function of these who occupy top positions in particular institutions and organizations. This suggests that leadership is something that is only possible to carry out if you are given a position of power and authority from which to act. Certainly many of those occupying such positions do demonstrate characteristics of leadership, but there are dangers in attributing such behaviour only to those so highly placed and extending the assumption to the idea that only those so placed are able to exercise leadership.

Theorists have approached the issue of leadership from many angles. A common one is to take a dozen or so outstanding leaders (by common perception) and attempt to extrapolate the characteristics they seem to have in common. This can produce a list of 'power behaviours' that seem to contain the clues to success. There is little evidence to suggest that this is effective in leadership training. Another false avenue is to try to tease out what it is in the personality and experience of successful leaders that may serve to explain their skills, abilities and qualities.

A more productive avenue is to ask the question – what is it that enables successful organizations to succeed and thrive? What emerges is a more complex answer than simply good leadership from the top. It seems that leadership is an altogether more diffuse concept than we have traditionally come to believe, that it can be exercised at all levels within organizations and that all participants are capable of practising it in some way. By focusing only on the behaviour of senior people we run the risk of losing sight of those aspects of human behaviour in organizations that leads to effectiveness and consistently high quality.

One useful definition of leadership is behaviour that enables and assists others to achieve planned goals. This suggests that leadership might have as much to do with making helpful suggestions as with making strategic directives; it might be as much about listening to other peoples ideas as about expounding your own and as much about gentleness as about toughness. What is clear is that effectiveness in organizations depends upon leadership emerging appropriately as and when necessary. Perhaps we need to change the question from who are good leaders to what examples have you seen of colleagues demonstrating good leadership. It will only be when we observe the qualities of leadership in our daughters and sons, the new and youngest recruits to our organizations and in the pupils that we teach that we will really be immersing ourselves in the world of leadership. Successful management of change requires multiple and varied leadership.

Management: Leadership

From the turbulence created by unprecedented change in the education system has emerged a clear but vitally significant realization – it is in schools, where leadership is clearly defined and exercised, that a capacity to strengthen and develop the educational experience for all is most manifest. A rapid increase in the rate and pace of change has altered the metabolism of schools, demanding an increased capacity to adapt and modify to new circumstances and environments. Schools, like all organizations, are undergoing radical changes in the ways that their business is conducted. One of the most significant of these is that leadership, rather than management needs to be seen as the most crucial focus for institutional development and growth in the years ahead.

This significant shift in emphasis will need to be accompanied by the re-examination of traditional assumptions about management and the ways that schools are organized and developed in the years ahead. Five particular ideas are central to this development:

1 Leadership rather than management contains the key to future success.
2 Leadership is a function of all participants in the organization.
3 All of us have a capacity for leadership and exercise it in various parts of our lives.

4 Leadership is dynamic and future oriented, concerned with improvement, development and excellence.
5 Leadership provides a framework within which human potential can more effectively be released.

What we are likely to see as schools work through the fundamental changes that are affecting them, is that success will be more comfortably achieved where changes have been supported by a radical rethinking of management concepts and structures and where all participants in school life have been enabled to identify their crucial and unique part in the scheme of things. Where staff have helped to play a full and active part in the design and development of the school as a learning enterprise, we are likely to see the most progress.

At the heart of recent developments in management theory and practice has been a radical redefinition of the distinction between management and leadership. The attempt to create a clearer distinction reflects a growing awareness of how organizations work, the dynamics of change and the psychology of power, authority and influence. Both functions are necessary and important and the following analysis is intended to be descriptive rather than evaluative:

Management is concerned with:

- orderly structures
- maintaining day-to-day functions
- ensuring that work gets done
- monitoring outcomes and results
- efficiency

Leadership is concerned with:

- personal and interpersonal behaviour
- focus on the future
- change and development
- quality
- effectiveness

These are descriptive distinctions and are not intended to imply that leadership is more important than management. Rather the distinction is intended to emphasize a growing understanding of the human and inter-active aspects of organizations. Management activity is necessary to keep the organization functioning efficiently, so that plans come to fruition, procedures work and objectives are met. Leadership is concerned with creating conditions in which all members of the organization can give of their best in a climate of commitment and challenge. Management enables an organization to function: leadership helps it to work well.

It is not a case of having either managers or leaders, more a case of being aware of the differences between the two and knowing when and how to be an efficient manager and when and how to be an effective leader. In most organizations these functions are combined in single roles and responsibilities, but it is important to be aware of the essential distinction between the two.

This shift from notions of management that are status related and role specific to ideas of leadership which are interactive, team focused, collaborative and future oriented is the theme of this book. Leadership is seen as a process which recognizes the futility of separating people from each other and which seeks constantly to find new and effective ways of integrating human activity, releasing skills and abilities and empowering everyone to a full and active leadership role.

Massive changes are affecting education at a time when the concepts, theories and practices of management are themselves undergoing considerable shifts of emphasis and focus. In traditional terms, the study of management has been the consideration of the discrete activities of those occupying senior positions in organizations. Within the world of educational institutions this has involved headteachers and their deputies. More recently attention has been focused on the middle management layer of secondary schools and the role of the curriculum coordinator in primary schools.

This attention to the concerns of senior management has tended to reinforce a class structure within schools, identifying the role of the headteacher particularly as needing special consideration. Such a separation upholds the view that those who 'manage' are somehow more crucial than those who carry out the fundamental activities of an organization and that their essential purpose is to control, organize and assess those placed lower in the hierarchy. In traditional manufacturing organizations, pay differentials, superior working conditions, more flexible hours, separate canteens, expense accounts and fringe benefits have driven deeply wounding wedges between the managers and the managed. It is significant that many of the new wave of information technology businesses are organized in totally different ways with few overt distinctions between the different layers of the organization.

In the professional setting of schools, this division has been less differentiated, with teachers being left considerable freedom to interpret and enact policies and plans determined by governors and senior staff. What has tended to happen is that heads have become less educator oriented and much more manager oriented. This has resulted in a much firmer distinction between educational functions and managerial ones. In primary schools, headteachers have absorbed an ever increasing workload of management activities and in small primary schools where heads frequently undertake full class teaching duties the additional pressures have been intense. In larger primary schools heads are often the only person available to deal with an increasing range of clerical and administrative activities. Having given up the educational purposes they came into headship to serve they are now struggling to hang on to the managerial functions in the face of increasing demands of daily events.

If anything demands high quality leadership and management it is the introduction of the National Curriculum. What has so far been achieved has been a triumph of improvization and expediency over planning and organization. If achievements can be created out of such adversity what might it be possible to accomplish given a clear structure of high quality leadership? There is little indication that this will be achieved through formal restructuring or even training. The government seem intent on creating many layers of management and the report of the School Management Task Force has only gone a little way to recognizing the particular challenges faced by those managing in education.

John Adair identifies five distinctive features in the concept of leadership:

1 *Direction*　Leaders are concerned to find ways forward, to generate a clear sense of movement and direction. This may involve identifying new goals, new services and new structures.
2 *Inspiration*　Leaders have ideas and articulate thoughts that are strong motivators for the working team, creating a directional energy.
3 *Building teams*　Leaders see teams as the natural and most effective form of management and spend their time in encouraging and coaching.
4 *Example*　Leadership is example and it is not only what leaders do that affects the others in the organization, but how they do it.
5 *Acceptance*　Managers can be designated by title, but do not become leaders until that appointment is ratified in the hearts and minds of the followers.

(Adair 1987)

Leadership in practice

For a long time there has been a debate about whether leadership is an inherited capacity or an acquired one. The confusion between the two was aptly captured by the referee who wrote of an applicant for headship in a confidential report – 'He is not a born leader, yet'. There is much evidence to suggest that the capacity to exercise leadership emerges early in life. The attention seeking behaviours of the new born child create responses from parents. This develops an early understanding of the relationship between cause and effect in human behaviour. In many ways children are excellent leaders. They have amazing capacities of bringing parents to behaviours that they are determined to resist. Who among us has not seen and heard the harassed parent say 'I said no, and I'm not saying it again', follow it up with 'Look for the last time I've told you you're not having any sweets', only to relent some minutes later and give the child what it was pressing for.

Leadership is not the same as manipulation, of course, but it is important to establish that all of us, despite our sometimes lowly status location in organizations do exercise leadership in a great many instances in our daily lives. It is not so much a case that we are not born leaders, but that clearly emergent potential is stifled and suppressed in the process of socialization and education.

In Chapter 3 a model of certain assumptions was presented (Figure 1, p. 32). This suggests that we are unlikely to develop our leadership potential successfully if our experience is a predominantly Theory X one. On the other hand, if we have been fortunate to have been guided by those extending a Theory Y approach we are likely to have developed a self-confidence that has enabled us to experiment with leadership behaviours in a variety of contexts and settings. Part of the new management paradigm is about promoting a Theory Y leadership. Such an approach will test the capacities of an organization to encourage the skills and abilities of all participants to emerge and to overcome the traditional struggle between control and achievement which has been so responsible for the repression of human potential within society and its institutions.

Another difficulty with the development of leadership capacities has been the preoccupation of funnelling students towards cognitive rather than interactive competencies. This is exemplified in the higher status given traditionally in schools, and repeated in the National Curriculum, to the elite academic subjects and the disdain shown for the affective areas – the arts, physical development other than organized games and anything to do with the imagination. Such a preoccupation with left brain development inevitably means that many enter senior positions in organizations with plenty to say about what should happen but with a disabled capacity to communicate effectively, empathize, encourage and inspire others.

An interesting angle on this problem has been provided by David Fontana who in an article entitled Knowing about Being (source unknown) makes the important distinction between these two aspects of personality. This can be summarized as shown in Table 6.

Our education upbringing and training has tended to emphasize the knowing dimension at the expense of the being so that we come into leadership roles incomplete and in many ways inadequately equipped to the challenges and demands made upon us. What is required is a balancing of the two, an integrating of what we know and what we are as a result of experience. Both aspects are vital to the expression of the whole person that a leader undoubtedly needs to be. Leading others is predominantly about managing our own being, exercising the multiple intelligences referred

Table 6 Knowing and being

Knowing	Being
Acquisition and application of formal knowledge and skills	Focus on the ways of experiencing living
External knowledge	Personal knowledge
Convergent thinking	Divergent thinking
Thought and action	Intuition and emotion
Second-hand experiences	First-hand experiences
Behavioural objectives, assessment and attainment	Emancipation from self-rejection and self-punishment
Outer behaviour	Inner health
Passing examinations, gaining qualifications and getting a good job	Pursuit of happiness
Quantity	Quality
The measure of our cost or worth	The determinant of our humanity

to earlier. What is missing from much of formal education is a curriculum for being; it is also missing in many programmes of management and leadership training.

Something of the difference between traditional Theory X perceptions of leadership and the more integrated and holistic approach of Theory Y is expressed in this story attributed to Tony Watkins entitled 'Rafting'.

By good fortune I was able to raft down the Motu River twice during the last year. The magnificent four day journey traverses one of the last wilderness areas in the North Island.

The first expedition was led by 'Buzz', an American guide with a great deal of rafting experience, and many stories to tell of mighty rivers such as the Colorado. With a leader like Buzz there was no reason to fear any of the great rapids on the Motu.

The first half day, in the gentle upper reaches, was spent developing teamwork and coordination. Strokes had to be mastered, and the discipline of following commands without question was essential. In the boiling fury of a rapid there would be no room for any mistake. When Buzz bellowed above the roar of the water an instant reaction was essential.

We mastered the Motu. In every rapid we fought against the river and we overcame it. The screamed commands of Buzz were matched only by the fury of our paddles, as we took the raft exactly where Buzz wanted it to go.

At the end of the journey there was a great feeling of triumph. We had won. We proved that we were superior. We knew that we could do it. We felt powerful and good. The mystery and the majesty of the Motu had been overcome.

The second time I went down the Motu the experience I had gained should have been invaluable, but the guide on the journey was a very softly spoken Kiwi. It seemed that it would not even be possible to hear his voice above the noise of the rapids.

As we approached the first rapid, he never even raised his voice. He did not attempt to take command of us or the river. Gently and quietly he felt the mood of the river and watched every little whirlpool. There was no drama and no shouting. There was no contest to be won. He loved the river.

We swept through each rapid with grace and beauty, and after a day the river had become our friend, not an enemy. The quiet Kiwi was not our leader, but only the person whose sensitivity was more developed than our own. Laughter replaced the tension of achievement.

Soon the quiet Kiwi was able to lean back and let us all take turns as leader. A quiet nod was enough to draw attention to the things our lack of experience prevented us from seeing. If we made a mistake then we laughed and it was the next person's turn.

We began to penetrate the mysteries of the Motu. Now like the quiet Kiwi, we listened to the river and we looked carefully for all those things we had not even noticed the first time.

At the end of the journey we had overcome nothing but ourselves. We did not want to leave behind our friend the river. There was no contest, and so nothing had been won. Rather we had become one with the river.

It remains difficult to believe that the external circumstances of the two journeys were similar. The difference was in the attitude and a frame of mind. At the end of the journey it seemed that there could be no other way. Given the opportunity to choose a leader everyone would have chosen someone like Buzz. At the end of the second journey we had glimpsed a very different vision and we felt humble and intensely happy.

This story is potent with implications for leadership and change. Above all it raises questions about what effective leaders are really like and in terms of the traditional paradigm the answers are somewhat disconcerting.

The new paradigm is not about denigrating traditional values and qualities but about extending them to include those that have been ignored and undervalued. This involves special and deliberate attention to these ignored aspects and a more complete blending of knowing and being aspects. It is useful here to reconsider the notion of multiple intelligence discussed in Chapter 3.

Power and control

One of the challenges to managers in an era of rapid and accelerating change is to contribute to the building of a new set of assumptions about power and control in educational organizations. Previous chapters have emphasized the debilitating effects of the traditional orthodoxy of central power and control vested in a small number of key people and the high status given to the supervision of those who conduct the essential work of the organization. The new management paradigm involves a significant shift away from Theory X assumptions and practices towards a proper emphasis on the capacity of individuals to be self-managing and self-regulating. Resistance to change is itself a symptom of the old paradigm with a retreat from dependency, oppression and control.

Traditional management and organizational structures in schools have tended to reinforce an external locus of control, inhibiting the full flowering of human capacity in both pupils and teachers. It is important to refer again to Frederick Herzberg's classic studies of human motivation. He found that people tend to resist change and appear demotivated when:

1 Those in management positions create too many rules, regulations and bureaucratic procedures for staff to comply with.
2 Managers exercise strong supervision and carry out regular checks on quality and output.
3 There are poor and inadequate rewards for work done.
4 There is low morale, difficult relationships, conflicting values and divisive attitudes.
5 The working conditions are poor with a lack of facilities and resources.

On the other hand, he also found that people tend to work with energy, enthusiasm and a more ready capacity for change when:

1 The work itself is intrinsically satisfying and challenging.
2 Staff have a decision making role and are involved in the co-management of the organization.
3 Successful work leads to a sense of achievement and the possibility of advancement.

The trouble is that so many of us have accepted the inevitability of the alienating and overtly bureaucratic organization that we expect to find

Table 7 Shifts in power

From	To
Power over	Power within
Power of	Power for
Power localized	Power spread

ourselves inhibited and sometimes oppressed by the structures of control and coercion. One of the new functions of leadership will be to achieve a fundamental power shift – illustrated in Table 7.

One of the keys to a more successful future lies in the raising of awareness about the forces and dynamics that are at work when people gather in organizational settings. Organizations like families are potent with difficulties and dangers just as they are full of possibilities and opportunities.

Working in educational organizations is doubly challenging because the educational process itself is a powerful agent of social control. Just as the management processes of a school needs to be built on a strong belief in human potential so too does the learning process. There needs to be a congruence and a consistency between the ways we manage ourselves as professionals and the way we manage learners.

In shifting power from an investment in centralized power and supervision towards a more empowering process we need to recast assumptions about leadership. This suggests that power is not a commodity to be allocated through allowance payments or bonuses but a resource to be released to mutual benefit throughout the organization. What often happens is that the power and control that managers exercise over their colleagues is personalized.

One way of looking at this issue is the idea of the Third Corner – developed by Alistair Mant (1983). This approach to potentially difficult interactions involves making the vital distinction between *interpersonal factors* – commenting on aspects of personality, and *work factors* – relating to work specific issues.

What often happens is that work issues are not managed or dealt with effectively because the interpersonal issues intrude upon the interaction, creating a dispute or conflict. We often find that comments that bosses and leaders make attack us as people rather than the issues at stake. This results in damaging and painful emotions such as those associated with being put down or attacked.

As managers we can try to avoid this by being very clear about the work issues and the needs of the organization. With skill we can avoid much of the interpersonal conflict that is often created if we focus on the work

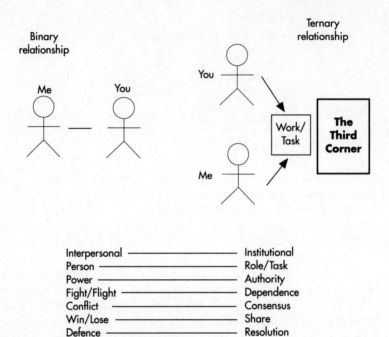

Interpersonal	Institutional
Person	Role/Task
Power	Authority
Fight/Flight	Dependence
Conflict	Consensus
Win/Lose	Share
Defence	Resolution
Raiding	Building
Status	Stature

Using the Third Corner approach in difficult and challenging interpersonal situations removes the need to defend ourselves. Instead we can concentrate on dealing with the issue and help to resolve the problem and the other person's difficulties.

Figure 10 The Third Corner

issues, that is the Third Corner (see Figure 10). The diagram outlines the essential differences between an eyeball-to-eyeball confrontation between colleagues and an interaction in the Third Corner.

To move to a Third Corner approach requires a truly collaborative approach. This will not be achieved if power is seen as a function of status and rank. Empowerment is achieved when leadership energizes the human capacity to achieve aims and realize visions.

Alistair Mant goes on to argue that the Third Corner is more than the work or task. People need authority in their roles, whether they are pupils or teachers. In well managed organizations there are clear and explicit constitutional arrangements which allow everybody, directly or through representatives, to play a part in policy formulation. The constitution is therefore another kind of Third Corner – an arena in which it is possible to have a sensible argument about what the organization is really for.

The relationship between heads and class teachers is interesting in this respect. For some the move into headship can feel disempowering and frustrating since it involves the giving up one of the key sources of professional power within the organization – the direction and management of the day-to-day teaching of children. Far too often teachers are described as having either too little discipline or too much. Rarely are they described as exercising inappropriate leadership, and yet this is essentially the management issue.

One of the crucial elements frequently referred to in the analysis of organizations is the presence or absence of trust, and it is central to the debate about power in relation to leadership. Handy (1976) illustrates the trust/control relationship by suggesting that the sum of trust plus control is always constant. An increase in leader power and control causes a decrease in the subordinate's perception of trust:

$$CONTROL + X = TRUST - X$$

But if the leader wants to increase the trust then it is necessary to relinquish some control:

$$TRUST + Y = CONTROL - Y$$

Handy further observes that giving trust is not easy because:

1 It requires having confidence in the subordinate to do the job.
2 Like a leap in the dark trust must be given if it is to be received.
3 Trust is a fragile commodity, like glass, once it is shattered it is never the same again.
4 Trust must be reciprocal. It is no good the superior trusting the subordinates if their trust is not returned.

But trust can be created if:

1 Participants are involved in the selection of key colleagues and have some say in leader appointments. (Sometimes found in task cultures, seldom in role cultures.)
2 The territory of trust is clearly defined for each individual and is not violated.
3 There is control of ends, not means.

Multilayered leadership

There has been a developing trend in recent years to develop within schools a more participative and involving managing process. Salary scales have regularly been restructured to reward leadership, coordination and various types of curriculum, pastoral and organizational responsibility. The 1988 Remuneration of Teachers Act for the first time explicitly formalized a contract in which a commitment to organizational management is an implicit part of all teachers responsibilities. The result of this has been to reinforce traditional hierarchical style management structures and to inhibit the development of more collegial and collaborative approaches.

One of the difficulties has been that of applying concepts of management and organization that exist in industrial and commercial organizations to schools. Inappropriate applications of some management theories to schools have resulted in a suspicion among many educationalists of the whole field of management theory, claiming that educational organizations have discrete features which defy the assumptions often applied in industrial and production organizations. It is unfortunate that some unhappy experiences have clouded the issue and inhibited a creative exploration of the management principles inherent in schools as organizations.

On the first day that a probationary teacher sets foot in their first classroom they are taking on the leadership and management of a complex and challenging organization. Unlike senior leaders of business organizations of similar size to that of a class of learners, the teacher has no management partners other than the pupils themselves, nor the benefit of a clearly defined specification for the end product. The charge of the class teacher is generalized learning and growth – an elusive objective indeed.

There has been a tendency among the management world outside education to regard schools as specialized organizations requiring little in the form of management, and seeing them as free from the demands of customers, suppliers, and competitors, although Local Management of Schools has imposed such concepts through the Education Reform Act. While there are some significant differences between schools and business enterprises they are not sufficient to be regarded as non-organizations. Some of the similarities and differences have been explored by Charles Handy and Robert Aitken (1986). In their Introduction they state:

> It is too easy immersed in the day-to-day pressures of teaching, to forget that a school is also an organization, that teachers are people as well as teachers, that children too are 'adults with L plates', all with their own motivations, with the same reactions to groups and to authority as the rest of us . . . kicking against organizational logic is not the easiest way to run an effective school.

What this book is promoting is a view that each class of pupils with its teachers also exhibits the characteristics of an organization. Each class within a school is a specific and complex unit within a larger federation. Just as in national and commercial federations, leadership and coordination is exercised over the whole, but the key parts are conducted at unit level. The key to success in schools lies in the achievements within these individual units and the key to these achievements lies in the leadership exercised by teachers in their classrooms.

Classroom management has long been seen as the art and craft of the professionally trained teacher. Yet strangely, initial training tends not to offer any significant management frameworks or theories of classroom practice. Curriculum models abound and schemes of content proliferate but the teaching profession cannot point to any significant schema of methodology to which its members would all subscribe.

What does seem to be clear is that some general management concepts may have particular relevance to classroom life and do not in any way threaten the specific and professional nature of 'teaching' any more than they threaten the professional skills of engineers, chemists or nurses in other types of organizations.

Take for example the analysis of management functions outlined in Chapter 3 and apply them to a school classroom:

1 Creating
   - having plenty of good ideas
   - finding new solutions to common problems
   - anticipating responses of pupils

2 Planning
   - identifying learning needs
   - planning learning experiences
   - matching work to individual pupils
   - anticipating outcomes

3 Organizing
   - operating policies and plans
   - taking decisions
   - providing resources
   - time management
   - being in front when it counts
   - recognizing when the job is done

4 Communicating
   - understanding pupils, their needs and behaviours
   - listening
   - explaining
   - getting pupils to talk
   - giving clear feedback
   - keeping pupils informed

5 Motivating
   - inspiring pupils
   - providing realistic challenges

- building self-esteem
- creating conditions for effective learning

6 Evaluating
  - comparing outcomes with plans
  - self-evaluation
  - measuring progress
  - diagnosing difficulties

All these functions are grist to the classroom teacher's mill just as they are to industrial or business manager's. What is often not appreciated is that teachers are required to perform as senior managers right from the beginning of their careers and what they develop alongside their specifically professional teaching ability is an extremely wide range of management expertise and skill. The phrase 'I am only a teacher' is a sad reflection on a profession which accrues management experience to a greater extent than almost any other. Shifting the emphasis of classroom teaching from a vague professionalism shrouded in mystique to the practical application of leadership provides a new context for initial training and professional development. If we devoted more time to helping teachers to become more effective leaders we might make real progress in education.

Given the range and depth of leadership and management experience that teachers acquire from the very first day in the role, it is surprising that we have been so guarded in employing these skills in the general management of the school. An enormous reservoir of management and leadership expertise is available in all schools if only we could recognize it. The criticism often extended to teachers is that of underestimating the potential of the pupils. We make the same mistake when it comes to creating management structures in schools. It is interesting to reflect on which is the more demanding management challenge – creating a curriculum policy for a school or guiding the learning of thirty pupils in multiple directions in a fixed time when they are all at different starting points. Yet it is the managers of the latter who are regarded as requiring management training in order to do the former.

A recognition that teaching can be interpreted and understood with the aid of management rather than pedagogical models may help to increase awareness of the enormous depth of management and leadership experience present in any teaching team. Grasping the notion of multilayered management and leadership is an exciting challenge for schools. What it means is that all participants in school life can be regarded as potential power sources in the processes of change and development. Leadership becomes a process of releasing and energizing rather than one of controlling and regulating. Self-actualization is both the means and the end of the organizational purpose.

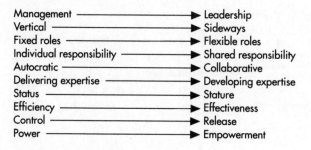

Figure 11   The Paradigm Shift

The paradigm shift in management and leadership

The 1980s saw a steady growth in the understanding of organizations and how they work. Central to this was a growing realization that members of organizations tend to work more effectively and efficiently when certain conditions are satisfied. Many companies began to move away from structures which tended to differentiate workers from each other and move towards more fluid organizational arrangements designed for flexibility and change. There was a growing recognition that the experience accumulated by workers in organizations can be used productively to serve management needs and that by increasing the management partnership, problems are easier to solve and change more comfortable to accomplish. Figure 11 identifies some of these significant shifts.

Management to leadership

This concept emphasizes that leadership is a human activity. There is still a tendency to use the term management to identify a particular group of high status workers in an organization rather than the process of getting things done with and through people. The phrase 'the two sides of industry' emphasizes this harmful sense of separation within organizations. There is an increasing appreciation that in most organizations all workers are managers and that no one is only a manager.

Vertical to sideways

Differentiating workers through many levels of pay and responsibility has been shown to inhibit the capacity for involvement and collaboration. Increasingly, organizations are trying to reduce the rungs on the hierarchical ladder and produce flatter more open and participative structures.

Fixed roles to flexible roles

In periods of rapid and accelerating change, like that we are experiencing in the late twentieth century, it is vital for organizations to be able to respond quickly to changed circumstances. When people are locked into rigid and traditional roles and responsibilities this is difficult. Roles need to have the capacity to respond quickly to changed situations and new demands.

Individual responsibility to shared responsibility

Effective teamwork is the hallmark of most successful organizations. When teams can be brought together to serve the needs of the moment quicker and more effective results can be achieved. Tying down individuals into separate and discrete areas of responsibility can inhibit the capacity of the organization to respond successfully to sudden change. It can also suppress the qualities of imagination and creativity that tend to be aroused when people come together in task teams.

Autocratic to collaborative

There is a tendency in many organizations to invest too much authority and control in too few people. This has resulted in the separation of roles and responsibilities. Flattening hierarchies and moving to more horizontal organizational structures inevitably involves a redistribution of authority and power. Creating a collaborative management culture requires that those in senior management positions learn to see their leadership role as one of empowering others in the organization rather than controlling them. Leadership then becomes a process of building and developing participation and collaboration.

Collaborative structures create more conducive conditions for skills and expertise to be shared and allocated appropriately and make it easier for individuals to be encouraged and supported.

Delivering expertise to developing expertise

Job related training and development is gradually replacing off-site training as the key means of extending skills and abilities. Many organizations are recognizing that in fast changing times it is more important to recruit staff with a high potential to learn and develop than with skills that may be superseded in the near future.

Good organizations help employees to see that career development is not exclusively promotion focused but involves development within a post. This requires an effective system of staff appraisal and high quality staff development policies that match the needs and aspirations of both individual staff and the organization as a whole.

Status to stature

Characteristic features of many organizations in the past were separate dining rooms for managers and staff, labelled car parking spaces for directors and names on the doors of senior managers. Such distinctions between 'the management' and 'the workers' have helped to create mistrust and resentment and fuel industrial relations problems.

An increasing number of organizations are working to reduce and remove the harmful consequences of these divisions and to create cultures which are more genuinely egalitarian and in which all participants are valued for their unique and special contributions. No longer is position in the hierarchy the requirement for respect; stature rather than status becomes the hallmark.

Efficiency to effectiveness

In recent years the concept of 'quality' has helped to place emphasis on effectiveness and to move beyond notions of the best product for the cheapest price. This involves quality control being built into all aspects of organizational life. Effectiveness involves a commitment to continual development and improvement and a constant striving for small but significant improvements, a process involving everyone in the organization.

Control to release

This signifies a shift in the assumptions managers hold about workers. The controlling assumption that subordinates are unable to work effectively without constant direction and supervision is giving way to the more enhancing assumption that all members of organizations are able to commit their skills and energies to the organization in a culture of encouragement and support. The task of managers is to create and develop such a culture.

Power to empowerment

This involves a shift from leadership as 'power over' to leadership as 'power to'. Skills of motivation and support are becoming more important then ever before and leadership increasingly seen as an enabling and enhancing process.

This paradigm shift is by no means simple and clear cut. Even when managers recognize the importance of more collaborative structures they are not always easy to achieve. Generations of the dominator culture have made workers highly suspicious of flexible boundaries and increased personal responsibility. Some unions continue to resist partnership and collaboration. The mistrust built up over more than two centuries will take much management skill to overcome.

Essentially the shift represents a movement away from the idea that organizations need to be designed and organized with the same precision and consideration as mechanical structures, towards an enhanced belief in the creativity and potential of people and their innate capacities to release skill, energy and commitment to the pursuit of corporate aims. Leadership becomes an activity concerned with empowerment and transformation.

John Adair has produced a useful way to conceive the leadership dimension: achieve the task; build the team; develop the individuals. This offers the twin focus of getting things done, and supporting the people who do it. Leadership is behaviour that offers direction and possibility but also responds to the needs that arise when individuals and teams strive to accomplish the tasks required of the organization. Traditionally, management theory has tended to place too much emphasis on the task and the organizational systems and procedures to achieve it and too little in attending to the needs of the people charged to carry out the work.

It is important to remember that leadership is not only a designation given to a named individual but a function which emerges in organizational situations and which can be shared by all those involved. Thus any member of the organization is capable of providing leadership in some particular way according to circumstances. Those who occupy senior positions need to spend their time not in directing activities so much as in striving to create conditions in which all those involved in the service can share a vision of what has to be done and work together towards its satisfactory realization.

Much of the pioneering work in bringing about this paradigm shift stems from the work of Tom Peters, Nancy Austin and Robert Waterman. Their various examinations of successful organizations have revealed some interesting and distinctive features:

1 'A bias for action' – preference for doing things rather than talking about doing them.
2 'Closeness to the customer' – managers keeping in regular and close touch with clients.
3 'Autonomy and entrepreneurship' – encouraging individual goal setting, decision making and evaluating, within a climate of change and development.
4 'Productivity through people' – seeing the staff as the major resource of the service and valuing their unique and individual contributions.
5 'Hands on experience' – insisting that all those engaged in management tasks are in daily direct touch with the 'nitty gritty' of service work.
6 'Sticking with the knitting' – not getting carried away with fads and fashions but focusing on the essential tasks and processes of the service.

7 'Keeping it simple' – few administrative and management layers and a clear understanding by all service staff of their roles and responsibilities and how decisions are made.
8 'Simultaneous loose/tight properties' – a climate of commitment to a central core of values clearly understood by all but within which individuals are encouraged to experiment, challenge, take risks and make mistakes.

In terms of how managers and leaders behaved in these successful organizations, the following characteristics of effective leadership were identified:

1 Managing by walking about – being constantly alongside the key staff.
2 Extensive use of small but temporary teams.
3 The promoting of self-respect among staff and the encouragement of peer group recognition.
4 Accepting failure as inevitable when it arises from good intentions.
5 Tolerance of ambiguity and paradox – behaviour is unpredictable and often untidy. People do not always do what they say they will.
6 High quality relationships with a capacity to celebrate success and confront conflict.
7 Inculcating the notion of development as the permanency of change.
8 Identifying paths for development but encouraging others to explore and map them.

Effective leadership is essentially an interactive process, focused on the creation of optimum conditions for professional creativity and endeavour. Further consideration will be given to these processes in Chapter 7.

6

Organizational cultures

Although a great deal of importance seems to be attached to the nature of the human environment in which change takes place it has not traditionally been the subject for much deliberate attention. This chapter considers the whole nature of the cultural factor in organizational life and sets out to provide some concepts which will help those faced with the challenges of managing organizational change in schools.

A number of writers have used the notion of 'culture' in relation to the work of schools. Fullan and Hargreaves describe it as:

> the guiding beliefs and expectations evident in the way a school operates, particularly in reference to how people relate (or fail to relate) to each other. In simple terms culture is 'the way we do things and relate to each other around here'.
>
> (Fullan and Hargreaves 1992)

Nias *et al.* (1989) use the term to describe 'the multiple social realities that people construct for themselves'. Westoby (1988) refers to organizational culture as 'social habitat', including the informal, ephemeral and covert as well as the visible and official. Essentially then, culture is about people in the organizational setting and is characterized by behaviour – what people say and do; relationships – how they work with and through each other; attitudes and values – how assumptions, beliefs and prejudices affect the formal and informal workings of the organization.

In cultural terms a school is an organization consisting of classrooms (environment) in which pupils (subjects) are brought together for the purpose of learning (object) through the direction of teachers (agents). The relationships between these four parts provides a very fruitful study for understanding why things are as they are and how change can and should be approached and managed.

Some cultures are implicitly stability prone – struggling to maintain the status quo in the face of demand and expectation for change. Others are stability phobic – anxious to avoid any sense of sameness or complacency. Most organizations live a life somewhere between these two extremes.

One of the keys to the successful management of change is a sensitive attention to cultural factors. Essentially this means trying to make sense of why people behave as they do; the extent to which their behaviour is culturally determined and the ways in which culture can be deliberately built and developed in ways that optimize the organizational purposes.

Characteristics of organizational cultures

As people we are essentially gregarious and our lives are conducted in a range of social situations. Our lives have meaning as a result of conducting them in relation to others – in families, social groups, organizations and as part of a wider society. Those who shut themselves off from society and live in isolation and separation from others are regarded as eccentric and abnormal. Being in relationships and in social settings seems to provide opportunities for a large range of needs to be satisfied.

How we behave when we congregate together in specialized groups in a controlled setting is an important subject for study. An understanding of the effects that organizational structures have on us is an essential prerequisite for effective management and leadership. As well as a pragmatic curiosity about the peculiarities of the colleagues we work with it is important to have some framework on which to base our observations and considerations. Nias *et al.* (1989) in their detailed study of staff relationships in primary schools suggest four identifiable features of a school culture:

1 beliefs and values
2 understandings, attitudes, meanings and norms
3 symbols, rituals and ceremonies
4 preferred behaviours, styles and stances

There is an interesting balance here between aspects of the inner world of the people – what they believe in and think, and the outer world of behaviour and interactions. This is a crucial distinction and one far too often disregarded when change is being considered and innovation planned.

In Figure 12 Johnson and Scholes (1989) offer a similar framework but build their model around the idea of 'the recipe' – the set of beliefs and assumptions which form part of the culture of an organization at work.

The six elements combine to preserve and sustain the recipe in relation

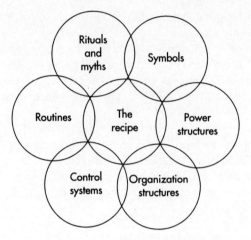

Figure 12   The cultural web

to changing environmental forces. The recipe, either consciously or unconsciously, is a major force in determining both policy and strategy.

Analytic frameworks such as these are useful tools for management and leadership. They provide important focus points for planning and action. Using the four elements identified by Nias *et al.* we have the basis for planning the essential first steps in any change programme:

1 Identify the values systems of staff.
2 Seek to understand the range of attitudes and values that are applied to organizational issues, the meanings they attach to their organizational experience and the ways that they make decisions about their own particular efforts and contributions.
3 Observe and note the contribution that symbols, rituals and ceremonies (both formal and informal) play in the life of the organization.
4 Observe the patterns of behaviour adopted by individuals and groups.

This requires an approach to management and leadership which is motivated by a healthy fascination and curiosity about human behaviour. People behave as they do for complex reasons which are not always understood by those who exhibit it, let alone by those who are affected by it. In management and leadership work it is useful to build the assumption that any behaviour, however awkward or bizarre it may appear, is purposeful, designed to protect vulnerabilities, satisfy needs or express feelings. It is not easy to understand these purposes and dangerous to interpret them on insufficient evidence. It is however, important to honour and respect them. The social experience dichotomy is a useful tool for guiding our attempt to understand. R. D. Laing (1967) has emphasized the importance of making a distinction between experience and behaviour in our relationships and social life. He observes:

> I can observe your behaviour. This behaviour then becomes an experience of mine.
>
> You can observe my behaviour which then becomes an experience of yours.
>
> I cannot observe your experience which is inside you, but I can try and understand your experience if you disclose it to me.
>
> You cannot observe my experience which is inside me, but you can try and understand my experience if I disclose it to you.

One of the great challenges to managers in organizations is to honour this distinction and strive to avoid the temptation of ever believing we can know another person's experience simply on the basis of their behaviour. We can hazard guesses and fall into the trap of stereotyping, both of which will inhibit the development of effective cultural leadership.

Decision making by managers needs to carry with it a certain predictability of success. The capacity to predict well is informed by the quality of insight and understanding created by attention to the four activities above.

Fullan and Hargreaves (1992) offer a range of cultural types defined in

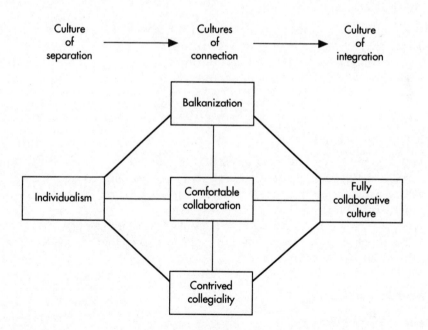

Figure 13   Management cultures

relation to their capacity for collaborative management. This model has been further developed in the East Midlands 9 School Management Task Force Project 'Personal Development Planning for Schools' and can be set out diagrammatically (see Figure 13). In this model it is useful to distinguish between cultures of separation, cultures of connection and cultures of integration.

Culture of separation

An individualistic organizational culture is characterized by:

1 professional isolation
2 no feedback to teachers on their effectiveness from outside the classroom
3 the school not being supportive of change and improvement
4 wide variations in teaching style and pupil management
5 habitual patterns of working alone
6 little attempt to build agreed and cohesive professional policies

Cultures of connection

Balkanization

This is characterized by:

1 separate and competing groups to which teachers are loyal
2 groups reflecting different outlooks on learning
3 poor continuity and progression in learning
4 squabbles over resources and territory.

Comfortable collaboration

This is characterized by:

1 collaboration not extending to classroom settings
2 collaboration largely at the level of advice giving and resource sharing
3 high participation in decision making, warmth, camaraderie on personal but not professional level
4 reactive rather than proactive planning and decision making
5 little contact with theory, reflective practice, professional involvement from outside the school

Contrived collegiality

This is characterized by:

1 a set of formal, specific, bureaucratic procedures to increase the attention given to joint planning and consultation

2 a preliminary phase in setting up more enduring collaborative cultures
3 a slick, administrative substitute for collaboration
4 collegiality and partnership being imposed, creating a degree of inflexibility that violates the principles of individual teacher judgement which are at the heart of teacher professionalism.

Culture of integration

A fully collaborative culture enables the expression of strong and common commitment of staff, collective responsibility and a special sense of pride in the institution. The staff indicate a commitment to valuing people as individuals and also valuing groups to which individuals belong. The examination of values and purposes is a continuous process. An open style of management encourages participation in the planning and decision making processes, fosters individual growth and ownership and creates greater responsibility and interdependency. Such a culture facilitates commitment to change and improvement, creating communities of teachers who respond to change critically, selecting and adapting those elements that will aid the improvement in their own work context, and rejecting those that will not.

The messages for managers, particularly those faced with managing change is clear. The cultural context is all important and deliberate attention to the building of an integrative management culture is one of the most important things school leaders can do.

An interesting and practically useful analysis of culture and change is provided by Murgatroyd (1988) who draws parallels between the dynamics of families and the culture of organizations.

He points to four styles of relationships as being especially significant in forming a cultural identity:

1 *Enmeshed* – in which the participants think and behave as one unit.
2 *Connected* – in which there is a strong sense of connectedness between participants, a respect for individuals and a high capacity for flexibility and adaptation to change.
3 *Separated* – in which self-interest takes precedence over the group, creating inevitable power struggles. Any change needs to be legitimized separately by each individual.
4 *Disengaged* – in which the organization becomes a production economy of independent participants and there are few personal or social ties.

Murgatroyd also offers four descriptions of the capacity of an organization to change:

1 *Chaotic* – in which the organization responds to change in an unstructured and fruitless way.

2 *Flexible* – in which the organization responds in a considered way with imagination and flexibility as events unfold.
3 *Standard* – in which the organization responds with a routine procedure and is reluctant to use new or risky strategies.
4 *Rigid* – in which the organization responds in a fixed way – usually 'No!'

These two sets of factors can be conjoined into the matrix in Figure 14.

This matrix can be used to anticipate and predict some of the problems and outcomes of attempting to implement change in different types of organizational cultures, and it is interesting to consider what would happen, for example, in an enmeshed culture with a rigid response to change. Trade union disputes of the 1970s give some insight into the difficult management challenges created when group cohesion and solidarity is combined with a single agreed response to offers and proposals. A separated culture with chaotic responses to change could be a rock band where individual aspirations become more important than the future welfare and success of the group and where the individuals cannot agree how to adapt their musical offering to changing tastes and fashions. On the more positive side it is significant to note how often failing or struggling organizations such as theatre companies or football teams can survive when under new management they develop a strong sense of collaboration and connectedness and a flexible strategy to the changing environment in which they operate.

	Chaotic	Flexible	Standard	Rigid
Enmeshed				
Connected				
Separated				
Disengaged				

Figure 14 Culture matrix

This model gives us a challenging and potentially powerful conjugation of connectedness plus flexibility as a blueprint of characteristics to aspire to. At the same time it offers a useful guide to diagnosis when difficulties arise and frustrations result from the process of organizational change.

Studies into the capacity of organizations to change and adapt successfully have stressed the importance of culture and climate. It is useful to be alert to signs of distress. These can include:

1 Excessive conflict not conducive to change
2 Excessive consensus not conducive to change
3 Repeated or unexpected poor performance in part of the organization by an individual or group
4 Low morale
5 Lack of concern among participants for their own professional development
6 High staff turnover
7 Failure of the organization to challenge and question its own decisions
8 Failure to carry out agreed and assigned work
9 Excessive paper communication and management by memo
10 High level of absenteeism

An understanding of these issues prevents unsuitable strategies from being advocated and unrealistic goals from being pursued.

Another perspective is provided by Miles and Snow (1978) who describe two quite different ways organizations have of reacting to a changing environment. 'Defender' cultures are characterized by a determination to sustain the status quo and pursue a 'business as usual' strategy. 'Prospector' cultures, on the other hand, strive for an innovative edge in the changing environment, recognizing the importance of flexibility and adaptability.

Culture as experience

In an attempt to provide a more person centred perspective on organizational culture and change, Gray (1988) looks to the experiences of organizational members as a key consideration. Such a subjective view he suggests:

provides a way of looking at organizations so that the uniqueness of individual perceptions is held in focus and becomes the major concern. Organizations exist effectively only in the experience of their members (i.e. those who experience them).

The purpose of the subjective stance is to understand how each participant experiences life in the organization and the meanings they construe to understand that experience. The management of change is seen as the challenge of handling varied and often conflicting interests, values and positions. Gray suggests two ways in which this can be done:

1 *Avoiding conflict* the organization seeks to avoid conflict by seeking compromises and reaching 'accommodations'.
2 *Confronting differences* the organization faces up to and attempts to work through the differences and conflicts affecting them.

Since compromises and accommodations are often those solutions which are 'safest in the circumstances' (i.e. they do not require substantial

readjustment of values or position) they fail to deal with the fundamental
issues, and change is cosmetic and superficial. It is interesting to note a
connection between Gray's two responses to change and the concepts of
single and double loop learning described in Chapter 7. Accommodations
are achieved when organizational 'discomfort' needs to be eased (single loop
solution) and conflicts are resolved when feelings are confronted and differences faced up to (double loop).

When managers and leaders adopt a subjective cultural view, they regard
the experience of members as pre-eminent and strive to create conditions
in which it is both safe and satisfying to face up to the difficulties and
conflicts. This requires a management stance which sees organizational life
as 'opportunities for individuals to grow and develop through the process
of self discovery'.

This suggests that successful managers and leaders are those who have
a strong commitment to their own self-awareness as well as a concern for
the inner world of their colleagues. The paradigm shift requires a significant
fresh attention to the 'felt experience' of staff and to the gamut of feelings
and emotions that are aroused by the dynamics of organizational life. For
too long managers in the interests of 'macho management' have been urged
to despise and disparage the affective domain. It is becoming increasingly
obvious that such a stance contributes to poor quality, low productivity and
inefficiency.

To provide a framework for cultural development, Gray offers twelve
propositions for consideration and reflection.

1 *Order and disorder*   A fear of loss of control is always a feature
   of organizations. In schools the determination to ensure control
   can be a major inhibitor to creative change, producing the resistance
   riposte – 'but we will lose control'. There is a deeply embedded
   organizational belief that chaos must never reign.
2 *Structure*   Structure is not pre-existent, it is a description of how
   people organize themselves and what they do to achieve organizational aims. To ensure order some structures are very tight and
   develop the assumption of pre-existence. A typical school example is the timetable.
3 *Intentions*   Organizations are created to serve a purpose. There
   are no pre-existent objectives. People create, pursue change objectives according to experience and circumstances.
4 *Determinants of behaviour*   A tension is created when managers
   try to drive by tight regulations and procedures rather than through
   interpersonal transactions which are the life blood of any organization.
5 *Individual interests*   Individuals always behave in their own best
   interests. Far too often managers claim that they are acting with

members' best interests in mind when it is clear that they are motivated by their own particular concerns and expectations. True self-interest includes regard for others, generosity, care and affection. It involves the mutual exploration of the meaning that collective activity has for individuals.

6 *Subjectivity and objectivity*   Organizational experience is always subjective in that members can reflect on their own experience but not on that of their colleagues. A key part of organizational development is about helping members to articulate and explore experience and the way that mutually experienced incidents can be interpreted differently. The sharing of perceptions and meanings is an essential prerequisite for successful organizational change.

7 *Reality*   Organizations are personal constructs, existing only in the minds of individuals. It is the sharing of these personal constructs that constitutes organization.

8 *Organizational change*   Organizational change occurs only as a consequence of changes in the individual self-concept. It is the individuals' view of themselves that change, not the organization. In managing change in organizations there are only people to deal with and successful change is achieved through the particular ways that the individuals change and develop their own interests, values and positions.

9 *Organizational functioning*   Organizations function as expressions of collective value systems and are inherently in a state of conflict. While it is behaviour that creates functioning it is the different and sometimes conflicting value systems of individuals that conditions behaviour. Managers tend to respond to behaviours when a more productive activity would be to help make explicit the values at stake.

10 *Causation*   Activity is generated in terms of psychological exchanges between members. It is not grand management strategies that bring about change but how at a deep psychological level members adjust perceptions, grapple with their own hopes and fears, confront their difficulties, acquire new knowledge and skills and negotiate new positions.

11 *Authority and leadership*   Organizations distribute roles and status without respect to individuals. In rigid organizations decision making is the prerogative of those in high status positions. In collaborative and flexible organizations authority is shared so that decisions can be made by those in the best position to make them.

12 *Management*   Managers can only be reactive to events, they cannot anticipate them. Management needs to be seen less as control and supervision and more as interactive.

The creation of this phenomenological perspective provides some useful pointers both to the sort of management behaviour most likely to achieve effective change and to the sort of leadership required to build a culture of flexibility and connectedness. In summary, such a culture would be characterized by:

1 An acceptance that organizational life is in essence complex, unpredictable and uncertain.
2 A capacity for collaborative policy making, planning, organizing and evaluating.
3 Leadership by wandering about.
4 A capacity for individual and collective reflection on experience and disclosing of perceptions, achievements and concerns.
5 Structures of critical friendship, quality circles and task teams.
6 A recognition of the centrality of the self-concept in all organizational activities.

Culture and change

A key factor in the successful leadership of change is the capacity to give deliberate attention to the building and development of an organizational culture conducive to collaboration, participation and change. Schein (1985) has observed: 'the only thing of real importance that leaders do is create and manage culture . . . the unique talent of leaders is their ability to work with culture'. As the pace of change accelerates it will be necessary to assist the paradigm shift towards more culturally aware organizations. This is not a task that can be left to senior managers, it must involve all participants at all levels within the organization.

Since there is little tradition of culture focused management, there are few examples and precedents of good practice to draw on. Essentially, effective culture building is a deliberate attempt to counter the iceberg factor. The iceberg theory likens the staff of an organization to icebergs in a sea. Just as nine-tenths of the bulk of an iceberg is below the surface of the water, so it is suggested, are nine-tenths of each person. Only the heads stick out above the water line, nodding and talking to each other in polite and distanced tones. Below the water line, however, the icebergs collide and bump into each other, sometimes with quite damaging consequences. For many of the staff in most organizations the real business of relationships is below the surface. Dislikes, fear, resentment, mistrust, envy, jealousy and anger and frustration remain submerged. What is needed is for the water level to be lowered so that these interpersonal issues can be exposed, explored and resolved. The superficial veneer of niceness which characterizes the human culture in many organizations is counter-productive and

Restricting forces
Work on these to
minimize and decrease
them

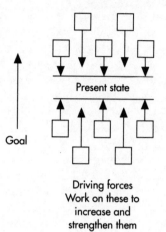

Present state

Goal

Driving forces
Work on these to
increase and
strengthen them

Figure 15   Force field analysis

damaging to effective teamwork, inhibiting to the development of staff and counter to the purposes that most organizations are intent on pursuing.

A practical way forward for those wishing to move into this area is to run an INSET day specifically designed to raise the cultural issues present within the school. This can be conceived of as an organizational resource stock taking exercise.

Further work can be undertaken by applying Kurt Lewin's (1936) well-known diagnostic model 'force field analysis'. This is a way of mapping the various forces acting on a particular plan or goal. It distinguishes between those forces that are serving to support the goal and those that are restricting its realization (see Figure 15).

The model can easily be adapted to facilitate the mapping of cultural characteristics. By selecting a change programme recently completed in the school it is possible to locate individuals on the map in relation to the different stances and behaviours adopted. This can provide the basis for further reflection about what particular individuals said or did to promote or resist the change programme, what range of values and attitudes were expressed and what influence was exerted by individuals and groups.

Although it is important to recognize the danger of using simple concept coordinates to analyse complex behaviours, conducting this exercise helps to make us, as individuals, more aware of the complexities of organizational life and the extent to which we are aware of the vital cultural factors that affect and influence the key decisions made.

We must always remember to appreciate Laing's distinction between behaviour and experience in our understanding of organizational culture. There is a key question to ask ourselves as we carry out this mapping: Is this a statement of observation or a perception about experience? Clearly carrying out this exercise alone helps to raise our own awareness but it also raises big questions about accuracy and understanding. For this to be complete it is necessary to have the observations and perceptions of all the others involved. The best way to use force field analysis is with all those involved in the issue under consideration. The purpose would be to map positions in order to increase insight and information for all those taking part. It is a useful way of moving into the explicit domain of culture and of significantly lowering the water table. The airing and sharing of ideas, perceptions, observations, concerns, fears and hopes is an essential prerequisite for successful change management.

Before a group application of force field analysis is likely to be of benefit it is necessary to find a safe but significant entry point into the explicit domain, enabling individuals to raise awareness of their own interests and positions and to hear about and gain insights into those of their colleagues. Using a SWOT analysis as a regular feature of staff planning is one way to do this. The letters stand for: strengths, weaknesses, opportunities, threats.

The exercise involves each member of a team or project writing down their reactions to proposed change in terms of the four categories. These are then shared, explained and considered. It is a quick and easy way of mapping the territory of change and of identifying the key issues that will need to be taken into consideration. To facilitate regular use of the SWOT analysis it is helpful to have ready-printed A4 sheets available.

Another useful tool to help build skills and competencies in culture leadership is the Jo–Hari window, named after its originators Jo Luft and Harry Ingham (Luft 1969). This is dealt with in some detail in Chapter 7 in the section on feedback.

The Jo–Hari window (see Figure 16) emphasizes the creative relationship between feedback and disclosure in the process of increasing self-awareness and encouraging growth and development. This suggests that managers need to be skilful in two distinct aspects: encouraging and supporting disclosure, and providing feedback.

A useful way of introducing this framework as a practical guide is to run a seminar for staff on its applications to teaching and learning and the development of pupil–teacher relationships. By extension the model can then be considered in the professional learning context and as a tool for leadership and management.

Simultaneity

Perhaps one of the reasons that the management and development of culture has been so absent is its tantalizing complexity. A glance at most daily

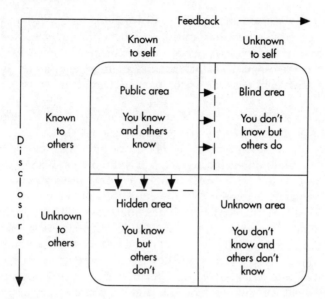

Figure 16 Jo–Hari window

newspapers will confirm that human behaviour is characterized by unpredictability and untidiness as well as consistency and inevitability. An insight into general systems theory will help to allay our concerns that because something is complex it cannot be managed. It is when we move on the basis of certainty that danger lurks.

General systems theory tells us that the world can be viewed in terms of relationships of parts to each other and parts to the whole. The parts are interdependent and the whole is the integration of all these constituents. A system is an integrated whole whose properties cannot be reduced to those of its parts. Koestler (1978) coined the word 'holons' to describe the notion that a system is itself also a subsystem of some larger entity. Thus a school is a system in itself but also a vital and interdependent part of the national education system. Holons have opposite tendencies. One is an integrative tendency to operate as part of the larger system; and the other is a self-assertive tendency to preserve its individual autonomy. These two tendencies are opposite but complementary and are an essential feature of organizational systems. In healthy and thriving organizations there is a happy balance between integration and individuality and the whole issue of culture is essentially the dynamic interaction of the two and how they create flexibility and capacity for change.

Effective management and leadership then is very much about appreciating and understanding the relationships that are played out between the different parts of the organization. Relationship is everything in a system and so in organizations it is a process of making as explicit as possible what is happening in these relationships and recognizing that all behaviour is a reflection of the felt experience of each member. Gray's twelve propositions become especially significant and an important part of our understanding of what happens when people come together in an organizational setting.

A further insight into systemic relationships in organizations is provided by the idea of *loose and tight couplings* (Weick 1988). This suggests that some parts of the system are in a tight and somewhat rigid relationship to each other while others are more loose and tenuous. Within a school a tight coupling would be between pupils and their class allocation which tends to stay rigidly determined for the whole of an academic year. A loose coupling would be between the curriculum – the defined objectives for learning – and what actually happens inside different classrooms of the school. While it is not necessary to define all relationships in terms of their apparent loose or tight characteristics it is important to recognize the complexity of the system at work. Human systems are among the most complicated, elusive and unpredictable and the process of managing them needs to be recognized as a task of the most intricate complexity, open to difficulty, disappointment, frustration as well as to exhilaration and excitement. It is in this context that the notion of leadership as high quality fumbling becomes so pertinent.

The important insight is that of simultaneity. An organization is neither one of loose couplings nor of tight ones: they are both and the characteristics are by no means constant. In their study of successful American organizations, Peters and Waterman (1982) coined the phrase 'simultaneous loose-tight properties' to describe this phenomenon.

They discovered that successful organizations manage the holon factor particularly well. These organizations promote the co-existence of firm central direction with maximum individual authority – what Peters and Waterman describe as 'having one's cake and eating it too'. In considering this apparent paradox they quote studies in the classroom which suggest that:

> effective classes are the ones in which discipline is sure: students are expected to come to class on time; homework is regularly turned in and graded. On the other hand those same classrooms as a general rule emphasize positive feedback, posting good reports, praise and coaching by the teacher.

The discipline of a few strongly shared values provides a clear framework within which people feel confident to work in their individually preferred ways, to experiment as necessary, to experience both successes and failures and learn from them and to know that at the centre of the whole organization is a set of stable expectations about what really counts.

Ambiguity and paradox

One of the great difficulties facing managers in modern organizations is the old paradigm assumption that human activity conforms to the same mechanistic rules and forces as the so-called natural world. It will perhaps take many generations to overturn the assumptions that have built organizational systems on this basis. One of the ways out of the old paradigm is to recognize and accept the inevitability that ambiguity and paradox are among the key characteristics of organizational life.

Unlike an object in motion, human behaviour in a social environment does not conform to predictability and neat equations. It is the hope that it will that leads so many managers to disillusionment, frustration and stress. An essential part of a successful management is the recognition of simultaneity, ambiguity and paradox. The fact that they have always been there is revealed in the collection of so-called laws that are attributed to Murphy: If anything can go wrong it will.

Heller (1985) observes that such laws and principles can simplify and trivialize, yet at the same time can 'convey with lapidary compression a notable truth'. He offers an alternative to Murphy in the Pangloss version which says: If something can go right it will. Pangloss was the philosopher invented by Voltaire who believed that we live in the best of all possible worlds. Heller also gives us Serendip's Corollary: If something beautiful exists, you're quite likely to come across it without trying.

Living with ambiguity and noting the inevitable paradoxes that present themselves daily in most organizations is an essential part of the manager's life. It was this feature that Peters and Waterman (1982) selected as the first of their characteristics of effective management. They quote F. Scott Fitzgerald who summarizes the point most aptly: 'The test of a first rate intelligence is the ability to hold two opposed ideas in mind at the same time and still retain the ability to function.'

In Chapter 3 the idea of multiple intelligence was discussed. We can now consider the notion of 'ambiguity intelligence' – the capacity to deal with inconsistency and paradox and the realization that complex problems do not have simple solutions.

Turbulence

Another characteristic feature of organizational culture we need to consider is the tendency to turbulence in organizations. In times of rapid change the presence of stability becomes a characteristic to worry about. With fast moving change and constant alteration and adaptation to new circumstances comes increased uncertainty. Living with uncertainty is uncomfortable, dependence on certainty is neurotic. In recent years a new area of study has given specific attention to issues of uncertainty, unpredictability and turbulence. Going under the general title of chaos theory it attempts to offer insights into areas which previously scientists have dismissed because they do not conform to the mechanistic and predictable paradigm. For most scientists the study of such issues was too dangerous to waste time on.

What chaos theorists have discovered is that within disorderly behaviours there is a vital creative process at work and there are richly organized patterns concealed within the apparent instability. While scientists studied the ordered formality of the universe there remained an ignorance about the irregular and erratic side of nature, in the realms of turbulence, unpredictability and eccentricity. Chaos is the science of process rather than state, the study of becoming rather than being.

In the study of organizations, chaos theory helps us to recognize that underlying the apparently unconnected elements of organizational life is a symmetry and orderliness at work and that we should never ignore or easily dismiss the possibility of relationships between one event and another. While we may not always discern the connections we know that they are there.

In *Thriving in Chaos* (1987) Peters considers how an increasingly unstable economic environment presents challenges to commercial organizations. He suggests that a revolution in management practice is necessary if organizations are to thrive:

> the times demand that flexibility and love of change replace our long-standing penchant for mass production and mass markets, based as it is on a relatively predictable environment now vanished.

What we are witnessing in education is a struggle to retain the control and predictability that sustains uniformity and central direction while at the same time watching the system disintegrate into a more varied pattern than we have seen before. What is certain is that the management nerve centre of the education service will switch from regional bases to the schools themselves. This will require vision and courage from those in senior positions and a capacity to accept that the future will not hold fallback positions if things do not work out right. The management of educational institutions will not be a job for the fainthearted but it will be exciting, challenging and infinitely varied. What this will require, Peters suggests, is that: 'we must simply learn to love change as much as we have hated it in the past'.

Psychological climate

Finally, in this chapter it is important to give some consideration to the psychological conditions necessary for people to be at their optimum – to have the confidence to make available as fully as possible to the organization their skills, qualities and commitment.

A useful starting point are the ideas contained in McGregors's X/Y theories. These are already referred to in Chapter 3. The diagram (Figure 1, p. 32) suggests that a conducive psychological climate needs to be inhabited with Theory Y assumptions about the participants' capacities to serve organizational needs. The control and command cultures of the past tend to develop and reinforce an external locus of control, stifling the proper development of self-responsibility, enterprise and creativity. The alienating dynamics of such cultures produces experiences of being dominated, manipulated and crushed by those placed lower in the organizational hierarchy. This tends to inhibit the self-concept, producing compliance with organizational values and aims, rather than commitment to them.

Building an organizational culture characterized by Theory Y qualities is by no means a straightforward business. Entrenched cynics and those carrying the scars of more domineering leadership styles may view collaborative endeavours as yet another, perhaps more insidious form of management manipulation. It will take much patience, commitment and care among senior staff to work through these stages of readjustment. Much skill will be needed as colleagues are nudged into collaborative zones of uncertainty, and much frustration will be experienced before a fuller flowering of human potential is achieved.

Leadership will be the key to cultural change and development. This will require the sort of approach described by Rogers (1967) in his considerations of the helping relationship. He suggests that to be successful in helping others we need to create a relationship characterized on the helpers part by:

1 A genuineness and transparency in which we air our real feelings and where there is no attempt to conceal significant emotions.
2 A warm acceptance of the other person, almost a prizing of them as a separate individual.
3 A sensitive ability to see the world as the other person sees it and to convey this sensing to them.

If we are able to achieve this in our interactions with colleagues then, Rogers suggests, the other person in the relationship:

1 Will experience and understand aspects of themselves previously repressed.
2 Will become better integrated and more able to function effectively.
3 Will become more similar to the person they would like to be.
4 Will become more self-directing and confident.
5 Will become more of a person, more unique and self expressive.
6 Will be more understanding and more accepting of others.

7 Will be able to cope with the problems of life more adequately and comfortably. 'I believe this statement holds true whether I am speaking of my relationship with a client, with a group of students or staff members, with my family or children. It seems to me that we have here a general hypothesis which offers exciting possibilities for the development of creative, adaptive, autonomous people.'

(Rogers 1967)

The successful management of change requires a constant attention to the organizational culture and climate within which it is set. This demands that leaders particularly are skilled in cultural analysis and sensitive to the nuances of human behaviour in an organizational setting. They will also need considerable courage to move away from the demeaning and dispiriting command styles that have featured so much in the past with such devastating consequences.

7

Frameworks and strategies for change

A framework for managing change

Given the enormous complexity of organizational life and the considerable challenge facing those involved in the management of change, it is important to develop some way of attending carefully to the intricate details of development while at the same time sustaining a picture of the whole. One way to help this process is to develop conceptual maps or models that show the key elements of organizational life and their relationship to each other:

> Such models, or intellectual maps, are more commonly used than might be expected as John Holt [1973] reveals: 'Like the economist, the traffic engineer, the social planner or the computer expert, children at play often make models of life or certain parts of life, models they hope are fair, if simpler representations of the world, so that by working with these models they may attain some idea of how the world works or might work or what they might do in it.'
>
> Good models portray with great economy ideas that can take many words to explain.
>
> (Whitaker 1983)

The model shown in Figure 17 is offered in this spirit. It attempts to capture the dimensions of organizational life and their pattern of relationships. Let us examine each of these dimensions in turn.

The external environment

Schooling is an essential part of social policy, providing a structured way of organizing the formal education of the nation's children. The structure

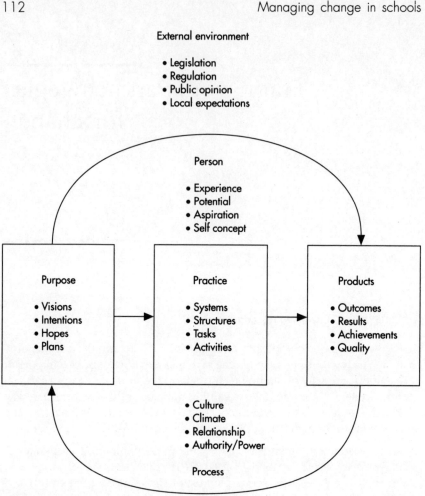

Figure 17 The organizational framework

conceived by the 1944 Education Act was of an education system centrally
directed and locally administered. In practice the active partners in this
process have been the schools and their local education authorities. During
the last five years we have seen a somewhat hasty disintegration of this
established pattern with central government taking a more controlling central direction while at the same time shifting the management focus from
the local authorities to the schools themselves. A restructured definition of
authority, with increased responsibility to governing bodies has created
some confusion about the powers and duties among the various management partners. The creation of grant maintained schools and City Technology Colleges has brought about a fragmentation of the somewhat monolithic
schooling system that had previously prevailed.

A fundamental part of school management is developing an appropriate relationship to the forces created by this changing structural environment. Schools for the first time in their history are faced with a plethora of pre-scriptions, setting requirements for their work and creating tighter systems of accountability. These prescriptions have a direct input into the *purpose* element of the model. Schools more than ever before have to plan within a complex framework of educational content and subject targets. How they assess their effectiveness is now subject to strict procedures and detailed criteria. In addition schools now have to take on a range of financial and administrative duties that were previously shared with the local authority. These environmental forces not only condition the strategic process of schools, they impact on each individual teacher and on the process of professional collaboration and development.

Less specific but no less forceful are the expectations focused on schools by sections of interest at local and national level. Parents have a major interest in how schools go about their business, an interest which is often confused by the disputatious quality of public debate and the partial stance of the public media. Public opinion exerts a strong influence on schools, both through its local networks of interest and through national debate.

> Public opinion is to some extent informed by the professional dialectic of teaching, but politicians, employers, economists, academics and church leaders also have their disparate opinions to add. In times of economic stress, education becomes something of a social scapegoat. As we move inexorably towards greater structural unemployment, the question of how we should be educating our children for a future which will be very different from the present, is bound to occupy those whose responsibility it is to decide the nature of the curriculum.
>
> (Whitaker 1983)

Sensitivity to the external environment is a key consideration for all or-ganizations. In commercial businesses competitive edge is vital to survival. For schools, the sustaining of confidence and credibility is the essential element, creating the need for effective public relations and high quality accountability. Schools will need to be alert to subtle changes in the climate of local opinion and ready to respond to fluctuations in expectation and concern.

The turbulence of change in this complex external environment is likely to mean that the 'prospector' approach to change management is more likely to succeed than the 'defender' stance.

The person

Chapter 3 has already provided a detailed consideration of the personal dimension in the organizational life of schools and Gray's twelve propositions outlined in Chapter 6 have offered a distinctly person centred perspective on school culture.

In the search for management processes which are truly integrating and collaborative it is vital to remember that all organizations are made up of unique and distinct individuals. A proper respect for individualism is a characteristic of an effective management culture and the leadership challenge is all about the harnessing of different patterns of knowledge, skills and qualities to the pursuit of organizational goals.

The model highlights four particular elements of the personal dimension. The first reminds us that all participants, pupils included, bring with them into school their own distinctive and differentiated experience as a rich resource for the organizational endeavour. The concept of human potential serves to highlight the fact that all of us can be more than we currently are, given the right conditions of encouragement and support. While ambition is often regarded as a somewhat self-seeking quality the important directional tendency in people is motivated by personal and professional aspirations. The more these can be made explicit and tuned to organizational visions, the greater the likelihood of potential energy being converted into a powerful catalytic force. The self-concept conditions how we behave and what we do. The successful organization is one that builds self-esteem and self-confidence through the appropriate balance of challenge and support.

The individual is the organization's most important resource. We need to strive to discover ever more effective ways of releasing the abilities and energies that are available within people and to create optimum conditions for personal and professional growth.

Purpose

Purpose is the first of the three strategic processes required to enable an organization to function effectively. One of the keys to organizational success is the ability of all participants to define and articulate clearly both the purposes for the specific role they occupy and the goals and objectives for the organization as a whole. This can help to create a powerful, directional tendency for all those involved in the life and work of the school.

In a fast changing world it is important to keep purpose at the forefront of management and leadership activity so that changes and developments in the work environment can be taken account of in designing new policies and practices and adapting to changing needs. Effective managers are those who are able to articulate clearly the aims and aspirations of the organization, both for their own purposes and to promote purposeful work and activity.

It is important to make a distinction between visions and plans (see Figure 18). A vital part of the process is the ability to project the mind forward into the future to visualize what intended results will look like. The

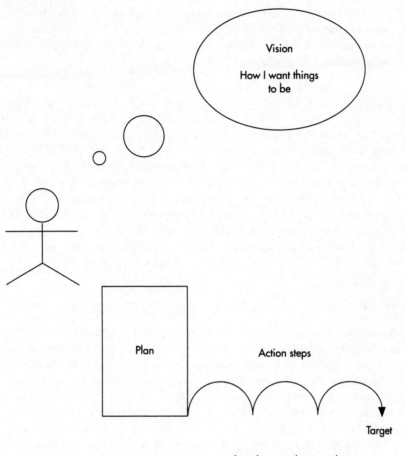

Figure 18   Visions and plans

greater the detail that can be supplied to this envisioning of end results and outcomes the clearer the path towards achieving them will be. The arrow in the diagram shows the important dynamic relationship between the purpose and the product: before we start the journey we want to know where we want to end up.

Peter Senge has suggested that the ability to develop shared visions will become one of the key disciplines of the learning organization. It will require a patient and painstaking process of involvement and sharing. Central to this will be the coalescing of individual aspirations and visions.

Visions that are truly shared take time to emerge. They grow as a by-product of interactions of individual visions. Experience suggests that

visions that are genuinely shared require ongoing conversation where
individuals not only feel free to express their dreams, but learn how
to listen to each other's dreams. Out of this listening, new insights into
what is possible gradually emerge.

(Senge 1990)

In recent years there has been an increased emphasis on development
planning in schools, with the annual school brochure becoming a vital
article of school information and publicity. The school development plan is
a vital policy link between the governors, the professional staff of the school
and the local education authority. There is sometimes a tendency to regard
the development plan as an exercise in accountability, a response to legal
requirements, rather than one of the key strategic processes of the school.
There is an important place for bold statements of vision, carefully formulated
through discussion and agreement between all the partners involved and
clear statements about intended end results, indicating that a school is not
afraid to nail its colours to the mast and specify its purposes.

Practice

The second strategic process is concerned with action, the transferring of
visions and plans into a range of appropriate tasks and activities. If visions
are to be achieved and intentions fulfilled, then enabling structures have to
be created and developed. While a clearly defined mission gives purpose
and direction to the roles individual members of staff occupy, structures,
procedures and systems enable the necessary work to be organized and
carried out. Management and leadership activities in this dimension are
concerned with the effective coordination of resources, particularly human
ones, in order to achieve consistently high quality results and outcomes.

Schools have a variety of structures and systems – the curriculum, the
allocation of learners to groups and classes, the distribution of resources,
the timetable and the specific roles and responsibilities of the staff. There
will be many informal systems, some of them temporary and short lived,
designed to enable the school to manage and organize its affairs systematic-
ally and efficiently.

The growing tendency in organizational development is to minimise the
inhibiting and debilitating features of sharply differentiated hierarchic
structures and attempt to create leaner organizational designs with fewer
status levels. This involves a greater degree of involvement of all workers
in decision making and the development of collaborative management.
Effective managers are those who are able to build and develop flexible
structures so that others can carry out the essential activities of the organization with efficiency and effectiveness. Management is the process of
enabling the personal effectiveness of others.

Peters and Waterman (1982) noted that successful organizations were frequently those which had a 'bias for action' – a capacity to translate clear visions and plans into success and achievement through activity.

Product

The third strategic process is concerned with assessing outcomes and end results. The productive school is one that succeeds in bringing about purposeful and planned change in its participants. The quality of management and leadership is judged on results rather than intentions. While all good organizations are concerned adequately to serve their customers' and clients' requirements, they are also anxious to devise methods for assessing and evaluating the quality of their services. This is equally true in schools. The Education Reform Act has placed a new emphasis on assessment and evaluation, imposing a set of tight requirements on schools. It is essential that schools incorporate these new elements into their own more comprehensive procedures for evaluation.

Essentially the review processes are concerned to compare outcomes with plans – to assess how closely results matched declared intentions and reflected the purposes of the organization as a whole. This requires, as the arrow in the diagram shows, a necessity to look back to the visions and intentions that were set. Effective accountability involves the accurate presentation of information about successes and achievements, and the clear identification of areas of difficulty and concern. The purpose of review is to bring about improvement. It both draws from and contributes to the other dimensions of the model. Management effectiveness in this dimension involves working at two distinct levels. First, with other colleagues to measure and develop quality of learning within the school, and secondly at the personal level, being sensitive to the effects manager behaviour is having on others.

The word 'product' is perhaps too material a concept for some, but it refers more to the process of productiveness than to tangible manifestations. One of the distinctive and challenging aspects of school management is that of defining outcomes and measuring quality. Senge captures this issue well:

Managing for quality in a service business is inherently challenging. First, service businesses do not produce a 'thing' whose qualities can be measured, weighed or tested. Quality is determined in individual transactions between 'servers' and customers, occurring literally thousands of times a day in a large organization. Service quality is inherently subjective and personal. It depends upon rapport between server and customer. It depends on how happy the server is and on whether he or she experiences the job as satisfying. It depends on the customer's expectations being met, expectations that might be neither clear nor mutually appreciated by both server and customer.

Because service quality is intangible, there is a strong tendency to manage service businesses by focusing on what is most tangible; such as numbers of customers served, costs of producing the service, and revenues generated. But focusing on what's easily measured leads to 'looking good without being good' – to having measurable perform-ance indicators that are acceptable yet not providing quality service. Work gets done but at a steadily poorer standard of quality, by servers who are increasingly overworked, underpaid, and underappreciated.

(Senge 1990)

Process

This dimension refers to that most vital aspect of organizational life – the way that people interact and relate to each other and the behaviours they display in the working environment and this was the subject of Chapter 6. It includes the ways that values and attitudes are demonstrated; how issues of motivation are dealt with; how power and authority are exercised and how conflict is resolved.

The culture of an organization is invariably regarded as the outcome of people behaving as they do. Developing culture and climate needs to be seen as an intention – the deliberate development of relationships, behaviours and values that are consistent with the declared vision. In this sense it is very much a strategic issue. Those in leadership positions need to recognize the central importance of organizational culture in their own management and leadership behaviour. Personal effectiveness in management roles is concerned with creating and developing the very best conditions to support the work of others so that they are encouraged to work to the optimum of their capability. It involves maintaining a psychological environment which is high in challenge but also ready with support. At the personal level, effective managers create for themselves appropriate work habits, an effi-cient work environment and pay attention to their own well being and sense of fulfilment.

In schools, organizational culture is important at two levels. First, there is the management culture within which plans are made, decisions taken and the work of the school organized. Secondly, there is the culture of the classroom – the climate of values and behaviour which so affects the capacity of pupils to learn successfully. There needs to be comparability between the two. One of the key themes of this book has been the importance of creating the optimum conditions for human potential to be released. One of the most vital tasks for school leaders is to work at building and developing these two related cultures into a cohesive and interdependent climate of endeavour.

This framework can serve practical management in a number of ways. It can be used as a tool for analysis. A range of questions can be generated to form the basis of enquiry and review. The more detailed the answers the deeper the analysis.

External environment

1 What are the prescriptive forces currently acting on the school? How are these received, communicated and dealt with inside the school?
2 What range of expectations are acting to condition the working of the school? How are these taken account of and related to the school's own expectations of itself?
3 How does the school see itself responding to an accelerating rate of change? In what ways is it learning to adapt to new circumstances?

Person

1 How is life in the school experienced by its participants, staff and pupils?
2 In what ways is respect for individuality of experience and aspiration demonstrated?
3 How does a concern for self-esteem show itself?

Purpose

1 What purposes does the school exist to serve?
2 What visions of the future are held by individuals and by the staff as a whole?
3 How are visions and plans arrived at, agreed between all those concerned and shared with all those involved?

Practice

1 What are the essential practices of the school?
2 How are the structures, procedures and systems related to the planned intentions?
3 How are tasks and activities defined and shared?

Product

1 In what ways is commitment to the process of review demonstrated?
2 What procedures for measuring product, performance and progress are there?
3 How are these related to plans? How are results fed back to those involved?

Process

1 In what ways do issues of organizational culture, climate and ethos form an explicit part of planned development, decision making and professional development?
2 In what ways can the school be considered to be a learning organization in terms of staff development?
3 In what ways are staff encouraged to undertake teamwork and to develop the skills of collaborative management?

The framework can be applied to a range of perspectives:

1 as a model for whole school planning
2 as a framework for whole school review
3 as a guide to the strategic work of governors and staff
4 to define roles and responsibilities
5 to build programmes of professional development
6 as a conceptual model of classroom life
7 as a basis for curriculum planning
8 as a guide to classroom organization
9 as a personal planning framework
10 by pupils to guide self-directed learning

Strategies for managing change

Engage and connect

Management work is relationship intensive. The key challenge is to create conditions in which all members of an organization can work to the optimum of their skills and capacities to satisfy task, team and individual needs. It is through the quality of working relationships that organizational success is achieved and change accomplished.

Managing change and helping an organization to learn the skills of adaptation is never easy. Satisfaction with the task is never full and complete but snatched in moments and measured in small but significant events. In the process of engaging with colleagues and connecting to their patterns of needs and concerns we must never set our own expectations beyond reasonable reach. Perfection is too expensive to contemplate, resulting in frustration, disappointment and guilt. We must learn to be comfortable with the unpredictability of human affairs. Leadership behaviours which are received warmly and with gratitude by some are regarded as attacks or intrusions by others.

As Gray has suggested, people construct their own organizational reality based on their previous experience and there is often little we can do to unfix it. When people experience the change process as difficult it is often because the experience of the present links with previous painful experience in the past. A backlog of Theory X experiences often means that we have difficulty struggling with feelings of being controlled when change is imposed without consultation, resulting in resistance. Those in leadership positions are faced with the structural complexity of a status hierarchy that itself can reinforce these Theory X feelings.

It is important to be aware of the effects that separating professional colleagues in such a way can have. Status and salary differentials have traditionally been the cause of a great deal of discontent and conflict, and the tendency in recent years has been to produce flatter organizations with fewer status levels. Hierarchies can create:

- feelings of inadequacy
- inability to express oneself
- inability to influence anyone
- feelings of being shut out
- increase in cynicism
- increase in destructive feelings
- feelings that one has either to dominate or be dominated
- feeling that to conform is the best thing
- feeling that intolerance and oppression have to be accepted
- feeling that new ideas can only come from the top
- feeling that there is no way to communicate with those at the top

People at the top of hierarchies tend to see their roles as interesting, challenging, unpredictable and satisfying. They have the opportunity to bring to their work the whole gamut of experience and expertise. On the other hand, people low down or at the bottom of hierarchies tend to feel bored and fatalistic, hemmed in and frustrated because so little of their total repertoire of skill and experience is involved in their work. Oppressive hierarchies tend to diminish people, make them less than they usually are and certainly less than they could be. Such a crushing of human enterprise is bad for the organization, ensuring a poorer quality of product or service than is possible.

Earlier sections of the book on needs and motivation and leadership have highlighted the strategies that can be used to help counter these damaging effects and create organizations of challenge and opportunity. The focus will be on the particular challenges presented by what are often described as 'difficult relationships' at work. These present a severe test of personal effectiveness.

While difficult relationships occur in our personal lives they are especially challenging in work situations and are the cause of much anxiety and stress among managers.

Few of us enjoy these sorts of relationships and most of us want to improve them since they can have harmful and damaging effects:

- poor quality work
- breakdown of communications
- low morale
- lack of commitment
- resentment
- mistrust

Such relationships are often stressful because there is often an assumption that managers and leaders 'ought' to be able to handle all relationships well. This highlights the complexity of organizational life. It is never safe to make predictions about human behaviour since most organizations are characterized by ambiguity, turbulence and uncertainty.

Many of us are used to ignoring the emotional effects other people have on us, and this in itself is one of the barriers to personal effectiveness. Without a high level of self-awareness we are going to find it difficult to appreciate the consequences of our own behaviour on others and theirs on us. Much of the stress created by difficult relationships is caused because we tend to hold our frustrations and anxieties inside us and develop feelings of managerial incompetence because we are not more effective. We may feel guilty that we have not been sufficiently forceful, or annoyed with ourselves for getting angry. It is at moments like these that we experience the loneliness of management and leadership and our professional self-esteem can be considerably reduced.

Effective leadership requires constant engagement and connection. Consistency of interest and concern is likely to bear fruit, even in the most difficult of relationships, and it is essential never to foreclose on any situation.

Keep listening

One of the tendencies in a Theory X approach to management is that the manager does the talking and the subordinate does the listening. An important feature of the paradigm shift involves the breaking down of this dangerous assumption. Effective leadership involves the optimizing of the human resources available in any organization. A constant theme of this book has been the need for managers and leaders to be sensitive to the needs and experiences of the colleagues for whom they are responsible and to help to develop their skills and qualities to the advantage of the individual and to the benefit of the organization as a whole.

Becoming an active and skilful listener is perhaps the single most effective way of approaching this challenge. Far too many managers look upon listening as an activity involving waiting for the other person to be quiet so they can have their say. Let us establish a working definition: *Listening is an active and dynamic process in which the listener attempts to gain insights into the perceptual, intellectual and emotional world of the speaker.* Defined in this way we can see that listening has not featured as a key theme in our formal education, nor unless we have been very fortunate, in our professional training. Even now the National Curriculum regards listening more as the skill of following instructions than the art of engaging with others in a relationship. Far from being a passive activity, listening becomes a very active and practical skill. The capacity to be an effective listener depends upon the appropriate application of a cluster of skills, as follows:

Undivided attention

This initial cluster is concerned with establishing the right conditions for an effective interaction. Conveying a sense of active attention requires:

1 an environment as free from distraction as possible
2 sitting reasonably close to each other
3 chairs set at a slight angle to each other without obstructive desks or tables in the way
4 leaning slightly forward in a posture of involvement
5 conscious use of appropriate gestures and facial expression
6 good eye contact

These actions and behaviours help to create an interpersonal climate conducive to effective interaction. They convey to the talker a sense of our commitment to the issues under consideration, of having time to listen and being interested and concerned about the colleague's affairs.

Supporting the talker

Once a suitable climate has been created it is necessary to get the other person talking and to encourage ideas and feelings to be expressed. The cluster of skills required here include:

1 inviting the other person to talk – 'Would you like to start by telling me how the project is going?'
2 encouraging the speaker to keep talking – 'Could you say a little more about that?'
3 using limited questions
4 keeping a sensitive and attentive silence

All these factors are to do with creating the sort of climate in which the colleague feels safe to disclose difficulties and problems as well as to share successes and achievements. Once the colleague has begun to talk it is important to keep the talk going so that matters that need to be brought out are done so. This means good non-verbal communication and some minimal verbal responding. It is sometimes difficult not to intervene and take the agenda away from the talker. Maintaining an attentive silence is the key skill to cultivate if this is to be avoided.

The best way to develop these listening skills is to try to change the balance of talking to listening in our working relationships. Far too often we use time when we should be listening to rehearse in our own minds what we are going to say next. Really effective listening involves an increased capacity to concentrate on the other person's interests and concerns. In conversation listening and talking are of equal importance to both participants. Many of our working interactions are more than conversations, often brought about by the need of one participant to talk through an issue of importance and concern.

Conveying understanding

This final cluster of skills involves conveying to the speaker a sense of being understood. This requires:

1 conveying a sense of acceptance
2 checking meanings
3 paraphrasing key ideas and concerns
4 summarizing key points

It is facility with this cluster that really makes the difference between active listening and merely hearing. When the speaker truly gets the feeling that the listener is really interested, is prepared to stay with the talker's subject and not to intervene in a judgemental way, then effective communication can be said to have occurred.

Active listening provides managers with a most powerful tool for leadership and development. Empowering people to go out and do what they are really good at is the key task and challenge of management. In the daily handling of working relationships lies the key to improvement and quality at all levels of the organization. A listening organization is likely to be a well-informed organization and one in which people feel valued not only for their contributions but also for who they are. When active listening replaces the oppressive and crushing behaviours that so characterized organizations in the past we will be some way to creating a working culture which brings out the best in everyone in a climate of collaboration and mutual endeavour.

This outline of the listening art focuses particularly on situations where decisions have been made to talk things through in a deliberate and structured way. Most of our interactions will be brief and more conversational. The skills of active listening are just as valuable here, facilitating clarity of understanding and developing a sense of connection and common interest so vital to organizational success.

Provide constant feedback

An important part of the management of change involves the development of others, helping them to extend their skills and competencies in order to satisfy organizational needs and to enable career aspirations to be met. One of the most effective ways of doing this is to help colleagues to reflect on their experience in order to learn from it. Providing feedback is a useful way of promoting this process.

In giving feedback it is necessary to be aware of some of the psychological implications of giving others information about themselves and their behaviour. Many adults have difficulties both in giving and receiving such information, yet feedback has enormous potential for improving skills, qualities and performance.

During the process of socialization, behaviour is modified through feedback, usually of the corrective kind. The upbringing of children tends to be characterized by corrective and controlling interventions by adults based on error feedback. Children are told when they are 'naughty' or have behaved badly and this information is sometimes accompanied by punishment of a physical, emotional or psychological kind. When children are given success feedback it is often because they have conformed to adult expectations and requirements. This pattern, established by parents in childhood, is extended in the educational system and reinforced in work settings through hierarchies of status and position. It is not surprising that feedback is associated with criticism and conditionality. Managers need to be sensitive to the background and experiences that have made people the way they are and determined their patterns of behaviour. Much will depend upon whether their work experience has tended towards Theory X assumptions or the more enabling attitudes of Theory Y. Among the behaviours and responses managers may encounter are:

1 difficulty in accepting responsibility for behaviour
2 fear of making mistakes
3 difficulty with uncertainty and change
4 assuming that 'others know best'
5 self-doubt and lack of confidence in ability
6 fear of success and reluctance to set personal goals for development
7 suspicion of 'experts' and those in positions of authority

Occupying a role which requires the giving of feedback, presents real challenges. Managing it successfully depends upon the application of some basic skills and strategies.

Feedback can be of three basic types:

1 *Confirmatory* giving people information that tells them they are on course and moving successfully towards goals.

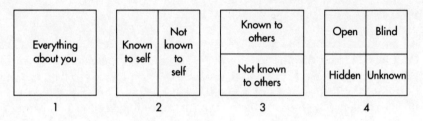

Figure 19 Jo–Hari window

Feedback of this type tends to be different from encouragement and praise. It provides clear and concrete information about specific behaviour and its consequences. After receiving feedback of this kind a person knows: (a) what they have done well – the *task*; (b) how they did it – *application and skill*; (c) the successful consequences – *achievement*. This information enables the receiver to continue repeating and developing the behaviours which have been successful.

2 *Corrective* offering information that helps others to get back on course when difficulties are present or things are going wrong.

Feedback of this type is essentially different from criticism. It is not concerned with passing opinion on performance or with designating blame. It is concerned with supplying clear and concrete information about specific behaviour and its consequences.

After receiving feedback of this type a person knows: (a) what they have done – *task*; (b) how they did it – *application* and *skill*; (c) the problem encountered – *difficulty*.

This information enables the receiver to modify and change behaviours that have resulted in difficulties.

3 *Motivating* giving information that tells people about the consequences of both successes and difficulties.

This combines both previous types of feedback and helps people to see more clearly the relationship between behaviour and its consequences. The aim is to provide sufficient information to meet the development needs of the receiver and enable appropriate choices to be made and decisions to be taken.

A helpful device to understand the processes involved in feedback is the Jo–Hari window (named after its originators Jo Luft and Harry Ingham). Figure 19 illustrates how the Jo–Hari window is made up, of known and unknown elements, producing the four distinct personality features in the fourth frame.

1 *Open* that about us which is known both to ourselves and to others.
2 *Hidden* that about us which is known to ourselves but not to others.

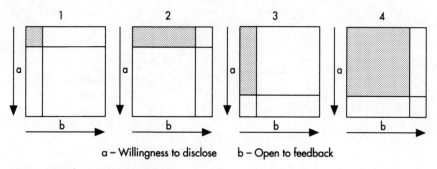

a – Willingness to disclose   b – Open to feedback

Figure 20 Jo–Hari window

3 *Blind* that about which is known to others but not to ourselves.
4 *Unknown* that about us which is unknown to both ourselves and others.

Personal awareness is increased and the potential for development enhanced when two communicative activities are engaged in: *disclosure* – a willingness to communicate information about ourselves to others; *feedback* – a willingness to receive and take account of information supplied by others about our behaviour and its consequences.

Individuals vary in their capacities to communicate in these ways. Figure 20 illustrates different capacities to disclose and receive feedback.

1 This example depicts a person who is unwilling to disclose and who is unreceptive to feedback.
2 This example depicts a person who is open to feedback from others but who is reluctant to disclose.
3 This example depicts a person who is willing to disclose but avoids feedback from others.
4 This example depicts someone who is willing both to disclose and to receive feedback.

The Jo–Hari window is useful in emphasizing the dynamic relationship between feedback and disclosure in the process of increasing self-awareness and encouraging growth and development. This suggests that managers need to be skilful in two distinct aspects: encouraging and supporting disclosure and providing feedback.

Our success in using feedback to build confidence and to develop skill will depend to a large extent on a capacity to avoid the recourse to judgement. Far too often feedback is judgemental – praise is positive judgement and criticism is negative judgement. Our socialization has been a process of being found fault with, and improvement has been concerned with correcting these faults. Too frequently for comfort this judgemental approach has focused on aspects of personality in rather general ways – 'You're so untidy', 'You really will have to try harder'. Such comments rarely provide the detailed information on which any form of improvement can be built.

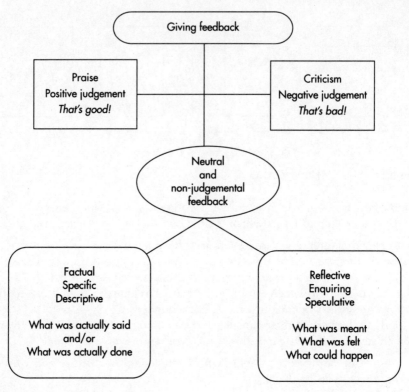

Figure 21 Giving feedback

The alternative to judgemental feedback lies in two different types of comment, both neutral and non-judgemental (see Figure 21). The first enables us to offer accurate feedback based on observation. This involves factual description of what happened – what was said and what was done. It concentrates on describing behaviour rather than interpreting or assessing it. Offered in this way feedback has the capacity to provide valuable data for consideration, leaving the receiver to relate it to their own perspective on the events and to make their own conclusions and judgements.

The second approach uses feedback as the material for reflection and enquiry and speculation. Here the observer is using specific, factual description to encourage exploration of practice and to engage in a shared pursuit of meaning and understanding. The purpose is always to encourage the receiver to gain insight into professional practice from which development can grow.

If feedback is to succeed in this objective, two particular conditions need to be created:

1 *Motivation* The person receiving the feedback needs to be motivated to improve and is therefore needy of the information which will help this.
2 *Moderation* The amount of feedback provided needs to be sufficient and not excessive. It should be matched to the perceived capacity of the receiver to take account and act upon it in significant ways. Feedback is essentially a sampling process, involving the selection of significant aspects of behaviour for comment.

In offering feedback there are four key factors to take account of:

1 *Be specific and concrete* This involves commenting on only those behaviours which have been directly observed – what was seen and what was heard. It is essential to avoid discussion or comment of what the person is like or to make comments based on inferences or assumptions. Deal in facts by concentrating on specific and concrete incidents.
2 *Be brief* Limit feedback to a few key observations that information can cause confusion and frustration. Start with one or two key observations and then allow the receiver to respond. In this way disclosure and feedback can work creatively together.
3 *Be descriptive* Stick to the factual detail of what has been seen and what has been heard. It is important to appreciate the distinction between behaviour and experience. The manager can observe others but cannot know their experience unless it is disclosed. In giving feedback provide factual description of behaviour but avoid speculation about the thoughts and feelings of the other. By offering specific and factual description we are providing information which invites a responsive approach to key issues and concerns.
4 *Be reflective* This involves offering information in a way that enables the receiver to respond through disclosure. It also involves listening with full and undivided attention to these responses. The key is to encourage the other to reflect critically on experience and to identify ways of improving and developing. Handled badly, feedback will tend to close down rather than stimulate the reflective capacity.

It is important to remember that change is a complex process. The purpose of feedback is to provide information which will help a colleague to make appropriate decisions about work behaviour and development.

Stimulate reflection and review

In the caring professions the term 'supervision and guidance' is frequently used to refer to a process whereby field workers are provided with regular structured opportunities to think through, talk about and review their professional work. Management work like many of the processes involved in professional care work involves the making of judgements and suggestions

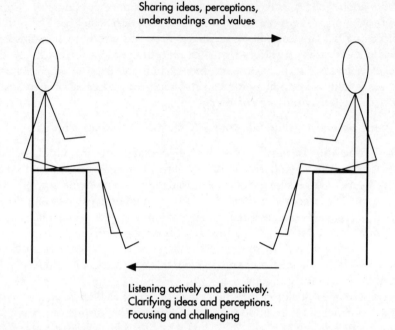

Sharing ideas, perceptions,
understandings and values

Listening actively and sensitively.
Clarifying ideas and perceptions.
Focusing and challenging

Figure 22   Critical friendship

about the lives of others. This can be stressful, demanding a high degree of emotional involvement in the processes of change and development. It requires a great deal of give and take between senior staff and the colleagues they work with against a background of complex variables and quickly changing attitudes and assumptions.

The allocation of time for work review is increasingly important in the fast changing educational environment in which teachers work. It is one of the few structures that has the potential to serve all three of Adair's leadership factors and sustain a focus on the six dimensions of the management framework used earlier.

Work review is a non-directed relationship designed to help colleagues develop professional skills through the regular process of reflection on experience. The concept of 'critical friendship' is sometimes used to describe the nature of this relationship (see Figure 22). This phrase has become increasingly common in the terminology of professional development. For some, the word 'critical' carries a somewhat threatening tone, particularly in the light of the comments made earlier about feedback. 'Critical' is in fact used to refer to a sharpness of focus rather than to any judgemental quality. The relationship is not concerned with friends who are critical of us, but with a friendship about issues of critical interest and concern.

From the leader's point of view critical friendship is essentially an active listening role in which the leader attempts to create a psychological climate in which colleagues can reflect on, explore and clarify aspects of their work experience. The process of verbal exploration and clarification facilitates a deeper understanding of the work issues involved and leads to appreciation of success, realization of difficulty and plans for improvement.

It is by taking part in regular reviews that we are able to keep in touch with the life and work of the school, to promote professional confidence and well-being in colleagues and provide leadership that will bring the best out of them.

It is to be hoped that appraisal will contribute the formal dimension to this process, providing a structured if only occasional opportunity to submit professional activity to reflection and exploration.

A vital function of leadership is to assist the process and practice of professional reflection and review. Reference was made in Chapter 4 to 'reflective practice' – the process of learning deliberately in and through experience. This is especially necessary in times of change when it is so important to apply knowledge and skills to the new and unexpected. The concept of the 'learning organization' was also discussed in Chapter 4 and the following equation put forward to suggest that for an organization to develop, change and survive successfully its rate of learning must be equal to or greater than the rate of change in the external environment:

$$L \geqslant C$$

Review and appraisal is the most obvious structure within which to develop this strategy. It is most unfortunate that the government plans and requirements for appraisal have placed so much emphasis on the accountability aspect and underplayed the central importance of professional learning. This again supports the old management paradigm of Theory X control and the notion that unless teachers are 'appraised' they will not perform adequately. Fortunately, the local education authorities that piloted trial appraisal programmes produced models in which the professional learning element was strongly at the centre of the process. The structural problem with the government scheme is that it becomes an event (a somewhat stylized sequence of activities) conducted every two years rather than a continuous and systematic process implicit in the management process of the school.

Continuous and systematic review facilitates the movement from single loop learning – the discovery through experience of what seems to work and new routines that can be applied – into the more profound double loop learning. As Day et al. suggest (1987):

While single loop learning is necessary as a means of maintaining continuity in the highly predictable activities that make up the bulk of our lives, it also limits the possibilities of change. It is argued that if we allow our theory of action to remain unexamined indefinitely, our minds will thus be closed to much valid information and the possibilities for change will be minimal. In effect if we only maintained our field of constancy we become 'prisoners of our programs' and only see what we want to see. Our rule of thumb decisions, once discovered, are rarely submitted to critical analysis, even though they may no longer be appropriate. This is an argument for engaging from time to time in what Argyris and Schön (1974) call 'double loop' learning. This involves allowing things which have previously been taken for granted to be seen as problematical, and opening oneself to new perspectives and new sources of evidence. Essentially, one has to be prepared to see oneself as others see us in order to better understand one's behavioural world and one's effect upon it.

(Eraut 1977)

When review is constructed with a double loop dynamic then it creates a number of opportunities:

1 Learning requires opportunities for reflection and self-confrontation.
2 Teachers and schools are motivated to learn by the identification of an issue or problem which concerns them.
3 Teachers learn best through experience/participation.
4 Decisions about change should arise from reflections upon and confrontation of past and present practice.
5 Schools and teachers need support throughout the process of change.

As Elliott observes (1977): 'The best way to improve practice lies not so much in trying to control people's behaviour as in helping them control their own by becoming more aware of what they are doing.' Reflection on the leadership of change is an important activity for any organization. Not only does it serve a vital cultural purpose – the identification of achievements and difficulties in collaborative striving to satisfy organizational aims and purposes, but individual ones too – the nature and effects of each person's leadership contributions to change and development.

Reflection and review becomes a process of documenting the journey of change as well as locating its specific outcomes. It enables individual activity to be linked into a synthesis of collaboration – the successes and contributions of teams, networks and temporary management liaisons.

Vary the leadership style

Current leadership theory is moving away from the idea that leaders are controllers, directors and supervisors of other people's work, to the concept of colleagues who satisfy needs, empower behaviour and respond to aspirations (see Figure 23).

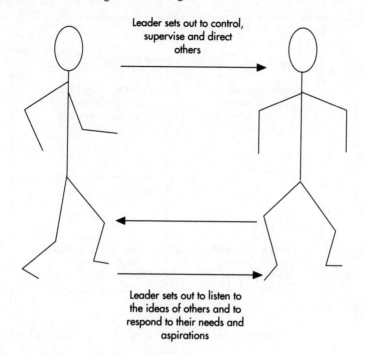

Leader sets out to control, supervise and direct others

Leader sets out to listen to the ideas of others and to respond to their needs and aspirations

Figure 23   The leadership stance

It is important to understand that leadership is a functional element of most jobs and a key component of personal effectiveness. A useful way to plan appropriate leadership strategies is to use the model devised by Blanchard, et al. (1987) (see Figure 24).

Leadership can usefully be considered as a relationship between directive and supportive behaviours; the balance varying according to circumstances and needs.

We all need different leadership support according to the situation. Ineffective leaders either use one style for all situations or use specific styles but inappropriately and at the wrong time. Effective leaders assess the needs of the situation and adopt the style that is most appropriate to the person concerned and the situation.

Leadership is highly challenging because people need each of the styles for some part of their work. When we take on new responsibility we may need someone to be very directive, giving clear instructions and providing demonstrations where appropriate. In those parts of the job where we are confident and competent, delegation works best. Under pressure we will need to be supported, and where new skills and tasks are involved, coaching will help us to develop quickly and effectively.

Both leadership and personal effectiveness are about judging the style of

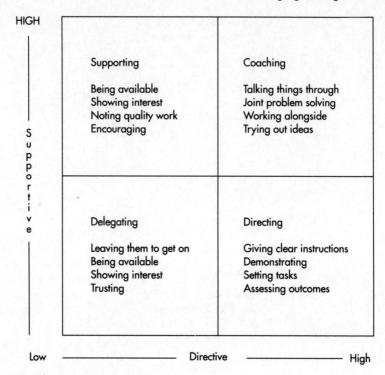

Figure 24 Leadership styles

behaviour that is appropriate to the situation and that is likely to bring the best out in colleagues. Not only do we need to be good at making accurate judgements about this, we also need to be highly skilful at using specific behaviours to satisfy them.

Walk about

Management by walking about has become one of the classic concepts of the paradigm shift in management. It suggests that managers and leaders need to see their main activity as interactive – alongside colleagues in the various locations where task work is being conducted. Effective leaders rarely call colleagues to their offices, preferring to take the opportunity to visit them where the real work of the organization is being conducted.

One way of expressing the distinction between management and leadership is that the latter is that specific part of management conducted alongside colleagues, face to face. Many headteachers have complained in recent years that much of their work is 'trivia focused' – a relentless pursuit of

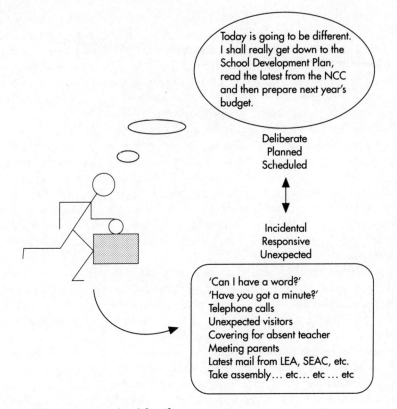

Figure 25   A day in the life of . . .

urgent but mundane tasks which take them away from the real work of the educational leadership.

As indicated earlier, management work is often perceived as a dilemma between 'high management' and 'low management'. Consider the scenario illustrated in Figure 25. This headteacher, frustrated with the constant failure to find time to deal with what are generally regarded as the important aspects of school management – plans, budgets, and strategic decision making, decides to take things in hand and exercise some control, so sets off for school determined that today really will be different. On entering the school, the caretaker approaches and enquires 'Can I have a word?' And so the day begins. Before lunch time has approached there have been frequent other interruptions, usually prefaced by the ubiquitous phrases 'Can I have a word?' or 'Have you got a minute?' By the end of the day the number of incidents have become too numerous to recall. Slumping down in the staffroom after the pupils have gone home one of the staff observes – 'It looks as if it has been one of those days!' It is only then that the head remembers that today was meant to be different, that good planning and assertive behaviour would have avoided the endless round of responses and reactions and the school development plan and the budget would, by this time, be well on their way to completion. The realization of yet another failure to gain the upper hand in the struggle between the urgent and the important produces an enormous wave of guilt and disappointment and a deepening sense of frustration and despair.

The dualism of this situation can inhibit progress and the discovery of creative ways out of the dilemma. The tendency is to believe that you should have either one approach or the other, and that one is the one you get and the other is the one you want. The truth is that the organization needs the painstaking policy making and strategic planning that creates clear pathways for development but it will only thrive and grow if the constant flow of daily issues are dealt with and attended to. A good organization is judged by how well it does its job not by the elegance of its policies.

What Peters and Waterman discovered is that the most effective leaders and managers are those who bring to policy making and strategic planning a deep and immediate knowledge and understanding of the organization at its daily work and that this can only be acquired by being where the action is and interacting with the people involved.

Rising out of the dilemma created by assumptions that policy making is high management and responding to daily crises is low management is not easy. There are many, education officers and school inspectors among them, who criticize heads for rushing around all day and dealing with the urgent rather than the important. This creates guilt and low esteem among those who seem to have no choice but to do their 'high management' work late into the night and at weekends. Such a view distorts reality – that most management work is interacting with a demanding environment and is not about lonely isolation from people and place. Minzberg's analysis shows that management by interruption is a highly effective way of operating, creating countless opportunities for real issues to be dealt with, policies to be highlighted, values to be demonstrated and visions pursued. It is because heads particularly are so good at 'low management' that so many schools are well run, deal with their crises and satisfy the demands made on them. A radical reassessment of this dilemma is called for.

One way is to sustain the distinction between policy and operations but to see them as essentially interdependent and symbiotic. Policies that are not implemented are redundant, operations that are undirected are purposeless. The two elements are inextricably linked in the system. What is important is understanding the relationship between them and the way that through daily activity policies and plans are made to work to satisfy the aims and aspirations of the school. Policies and plans need to reflect the reality of organizational life and operations need to be managed to pursue declared aims. Part of organizational reality is an increasing rate of change that creates turbulence and uncertainty and increases the amount of interactive activity that needs to be undertaken to respond to it. Change creates questions, uncertainties, anxieties, arguments, mistakes and misunderstandings. Only leadership of the highest quality can sustain organizational well-being and self-esteem and enable the organization to succeed.

Policy making and strategic planning are not essentially tasks for headteachers, heads of department and curriculum leaders to conduct in lonely isolation. They are the concern of the whole organization and best tackled collaboratively by task teams. It is at the operational level that opportunities for leadership really exist. Every incident, event, problem or 'crisis' during a school day is a golden opportunity to exercise leadership and serve the aims and aspirations contained in policies and plans. A simple checklist will help to indicate what most organizational leaders should be doing most of the time:

1 identifying needs in individuals and teams
2 responding to queries, questions, comments
3 solving problems, difficulties
4 building relationships
5 noticing and rewarding achievements throughout the organization
6 listening to the experience of individuals
7 pursuing visions and plans
8 increasing motivation
9 making small but significant improvements
10 communicating constantly

Since virtually all the incidents and events in a typical day will be created by people, they can only be dealt with interactively, sometimes face to face and sometimes on the telephone. Such interactive leadership requires sensitivity, understanding, empathy, wisdom and courage.

Henry Minzberg in his detailed studies of managers' work found that far from engaging in a series of grand strategic activities, leadership work was characterized by constant interruption. Half of their activities last nine minutes or less and only ten per cent exceeded one hour. Minzberg suggests that it is the immediacy and spontaneity of so much management work that is one of its chief attractions:

> The traditional literature notwithstanding, the job of managing does not breed reflective planners; the manager responds to stimuli as an individual who is conditioned by the job to prefer live to delayed action.
>
> (Minzberg 1973)

In the twenty years or so since these studies were undertaken there has been an increased focus on strategic planning, creating a dilemma in the minds of many managers – keeping alongside the people conducting the real business of the organization, or separating themselves from the action to engage in the articulation of policies and plans.

It is only by getting to know the colleagues that we are responsible for that we are able to provide appropriate leadership. This requires us to be with them from time to time, taking an interest, encouraging and supporting.

Encourage collaboration

The chapter on organizational cultures has emphasized how important it is to involve everyone in the working venture. Through involvement and collaboration it is possible to maximize the human resources and skills, commitment and energy to create a potent and catalytic mix for successful change and development. The paradigm shift in management is concerned with a move away from the tragedy of separation in organizations – which results in the isolating of individuals into a distinctive and different realm of responsibility, and the imposition of line management structures to rein-force the Theory X approach to the management of work.

There is an excitement in integration of effort. When people come to-gether to serve aims and purposes to which they are mutually committed then synergy seems to be created, increasing possibilities and making for quality. The way ahead will depend upon collaboration through the cre-ation of new and changing management partnerships within organizations. This will depend upon a capacity of the most senior staff to redefine the nature of authority and power within the organization and to build a new assumption that management and leadership are integral processes, part of the responsibility of everyone.

While senior managers will occupy a key role in facilitating the critical path through the various phases of policy making, all staff need to feel a sense of ownership and commitment to the process and its anticipated end results. Good teamwork results when there is a high capacity to distinguish between the task skills of managing policy, strategy and operations and the process of managerial skills which facilitate them. Attention to the process skills often enables the vital task skills of the group to be released. Awareness of and attention to the process of working together can affect the outcomes and results in a very positive way. When there is a preoccupation with the task it can be difficult to notice the poor processes inhibiting group cohesion.

Within educational organizations there are a number of challenges to collaborative management:

1 the problem of equitable responsibility
2 the difficulty of creating a sense of shared responsibility

3 the issue of salary differentials
4 the question of accountability

Schools where effective teamwork operates have usually succeeded in ameliorating the inhibiting features of the traditional hierarchical structure in favour of a more collegial approach.

Improve delegation

Within most organizations people are arranged in a hierarchy with differen-tiated functions and responsibilities. Work is distributed through the levels by the process of delegation. Most managers are involved in this process, often working in two directions – upwards to senior colleagues, and down-wards to those for whom they have responsibility. A key component of personal effectiveness in the management role is handling delegation well.

Management has been defined as the process of getting things done with and through other people. This involves sharing the work out so that all those involved are able to work within the area of their responsibility to the optimum of their skill and capacity.

Delegation serves two purposes: it enables a manager to share tasks and activities with others, and it helps in the development of skills and abilities in those to whom work is delegated, enabling them to take on progressively more complex and challenging work.

There is often confusion about what is involved in the process of delega-tion. It is far more than the simple allocation of tasks. It involves the cre-ation and development of relationships of trust so that effective results are achieved and individuals are afforded appropriate challenge and support.

Apart from the fact that delegation distributes work between staff there are other benefits. People will tend to respect and value those who are able to bring out the best in them. The more that is delegated within clear boundaries of responsibility the more individuals have freedom to interpret and manage the job for themselves and the less management time is then required to supervise them. Freedom from supervision also allows people the many benefits of self-management: increased job satisfaction, greater energy, higher morale, greater self-respect.

The cost of delegation is the increased risk that freedom entails. The more freedom that is given to people then the greater the likelihood of mistakes. The skill in delegation involves making sure that these mistakes are affordable and necessary to the development of skills and abilities.

Effective delegation involves not asking people to accept more respons-ibility than is required at their particular job level and not giving more authority than is appropriate. In managing delegation the watchwords are: 'Hands off as much as possible and hands on as much as necessary' (Blanchard *et al.* 1990).

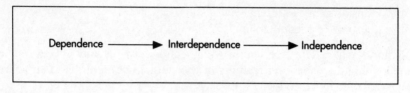

Figure 26 The journey from dependency

The aim is to balance the individual's desire for freedom with the organization's need for protection. Far too often the concern for the latter results in a stifling of the first.

Responsibility

In successful organizations responsibilities are spread throughout the workforce. A vital factor in this interdependent system is the need for each member of the organization to work fully within the bounds of their responsibility.

Having the capacity to take responsibility is achieved when a climate of trust is created. Those in management positions need to provide the sort of leadership that enables colleagues both to accept responsibility and to exercise it. This relationship is developed through experience. The sequence shown in Figure 26 is useful in understanding the process of management involved in delegation.

Dependence

People new to a job tend to have a great deal of dependence on their line manager. For some parts of the job this dependence is short lived and once the new colleague has 'learnt the ropes' is well able to get on, with only occasional references for advice and information. Dependence is likely to remain if the job is a developmental one, involving progressively more demanding tasks as experience is acquired and competence developed.

Interdependence

This is the ideal relationship between a worker and a line manager. Both are partners in a job or task. Interactions arise when the manager needs to check on progress and development and when the colleague needs to report or consult about specific issues.

Independence

Some parts of the colleague's job will be characterized by a clear capacity to self-manage without supervision. An important managerial skill is recognizing these parts of their colleagues' work and resisting the temptation to interfere or over-supervise.

All three of these elements are present in all jobs. Delegation is the process of recognizing them and behaving appropriately.

Confidence

Building relationships of mutual trust involves having confidence in each other.

The manager needs to feel:

- this colleague is up to the job
- he/she has the skills to do the job well
- he/she has a proven track record of effectiveness
- he/she delivers on time
- he/she is well able to handle the responsibility

The colleague needs to feel:

- my manager shows confidence in my abilities
- he/she provides a clear brief for the task or project
- he/she makes very clear the nature and extent of my authority
- he/she spells out boundaries, specifications and deadlines
- he/she provides a full and regular flow of information
- he/she leaves me to get on with it but is available for consultation

Developing confidence in each other is not an accidental process. It needs to be worked at and progress made by reviewing experience and learning from it. The confidence points listed above can be used as a checklist and made the subject of review discussions between colleagues in line management relationships.

Uncertainty and confusion

One of the key problems in delegation is the tendency for managers to undertake themselves work they should delegate. This is often the case where they have been promoted to become the manager of the job they once did. One of the key messages for managers is: Stop doing the job you have been promoted from and start doing the job you have been promoted to.

Managers present many arguments for not heeding this advice:

- 'If you want a job done well, do it yourself.'
- 'This one is too hot for my staff to handle.'
- 'I want to keep my hand in.'
- 'It's easier to do it yourself than to delegate it.'
- 'I don't want to ask my staff to do anything I'm not willing to do myself.'

It is not surprising that so many of us are under pressure, claiming we never have time to get everything done.

Expect the unexpected

One of the essential attractions of management and change is the largely unpredictable nature of the work. While there will be times when things seem to be going according to plan it is likely that the change process will be characterized by confusions, concerns, anxieties, teething troubles and occasionally major setbacks. These are grist to the creative leader's mill and much to be relished, providing key opportunities to engage at the heart of the process. Good leaders are at their best when the going gets tough, when frustration with slow progress wells up, when essential resources are not forthcoming and when unexpected obstacles present themselves. It is for occasions such as these that leadership carries a salary differential. Quality leadership here requires keeping purposes and visions in focus, creating new structures and strategies to enable corrective action to be taken and judging when things are back on course. The model presented earlier in the chapter provides a useful map to the challenging tasks of problem solving, strategic adjustment and motivation. It offers a ground plan for guiding the subtle but challenging work of managing change.

8
Challenges for the future

The previous chapters of this book have considered a range of approaches to the managing of change in schools. Together they emphasize the need to shift our assumptions about the nature of change and to see it, not in terms of strategic events and incidents, but as a process of continuous adjustment, development and improvement. For those in senior positions in schools this will require a quality of leadership that has not been needed before but which will be essential in the future. Leaders will need to help their colleagues to learn to love change as much as they have valued certainty. The challenge is to assist in bringing about a new organizational metabolism, more creative, more adaptive and more self-assertive than in the past.

For leaders themselves this may seem a daunting task for it means that most of all they will have to be fascinated with change and comfortable in confusion. In a world where flexibility is strength, the challenge to personal equanimity comes through learning to expect ambiguity, working confidently in complexity and operating creatively in flux. Peters sums it up well: 'Today, loving change, tumult, even chaos is a prerequisite for survival, let alone success' (Peters 1988).

This chapter will consider these challenges in three particular ways. First, by outlining the development needs of those whose roles and responsibilities place them at the edge of change, striving to help their schools adapt successfully to a fast changing world. Secondly, it will explore the concept of quality in relation to the management of change in schools. Thirdly, it will attempt to offer some positive and comforting ideas on the theme of chaos.

A process of becoming

Of fundamental importance in the changed and changing world of the future will be the capacity of those in leadership and management positions to care for and foster their own development and change. This will demand a proper selfishness in which time for personal reflection and thinking is not seen as an indulgence but as a top priority. It will not be enough to put the sign 'please do not disturb' on the outside of our doors, it will be necessary to hang it round our necks. Being busy will not be measured by the speed of our actions but by the intensity of the quietness and calm that we can bring to the reflective process.

In Chapter 4 the concept of the reflective practitioner was considered. The capacity to cope with increasing complexity and confusion will require more personal thinking and somewhat less action. It is vital to change the appalling assumption prevalent in our society that people who sit and think are doing nothing. Reclaiming the importance of stillness, quietness and contemplation is a matter of some urgency. No longer should anyone feel guilty if they are 'caught napping'. Research has shown that our thinking processes can often work better when we achieve a state of inner calm and stillness. Some organizations, aware of the importance of releasing the higher thinking skills of their people are creating quiet times inside their busy schedules and modifying their building design to form places to which people can go if they want uninterrupted thinking time, although some employers, ever mistrustful, will see this as an opportunity for 'skiving' and so Theory X will prevail.

It is important to recognize a wide variation of thinking styles among different people. Some have their best ideas when walking in the hills, others when sitting quietly with music playing in the background. Organizations which recognize that it is the creativity and imagination of their people that they are paying for will invest heavily in creating the optimum conditions for thinking and reflection to flourish.

Success in leadership will depend too upon the recognition that organizational goals are ephemeral, often only staging posts on much longer journeys. Arriving becomes a temporary experience as changed circumstances demand new departures. A concern with ends should be accompanied by a commitment to movement and reaching out. Professional development is not a precise preparation for anticipated events, but a process of constant self-renewal. The pursuit of a way of being becomes a dedication to a process of becoming in which the journey itself is the destination.

One of the most challenging demands to self-development will be to the inner personal world of thinking, feeling and intuition. Fixed ideas and habitual patterns of thought will need to be disturbed in the struggle to discover new ways of approaching problems. It will be more necessary than ever to struggle out of the bondage of those forms of pernicious thinking that so often limit and hinder our efforts to achieve. It is essential that we increase self-awareness and recognize the many different ways through which experience has formed our personalities and conditioned our behaviour.

Transactional Analysis emphasizes how powerful early childhood experience is in establishing personality traits and forming patterns of interpersonal behaviour. In its analysis of personality and through its theories of relationships and interactions Transactional Analysis offers a range of insights that can help us in this process of increasing self-awareness. Many will be familiar with the three ego states – Parent, Adult and Child – which serve to explain interpersonal behaviour in relationships. Of particular interest in the context of leadership are the set of negative restrictive messages conveyed from parents to children during childhood. These 'drivers' become internalized through experience and tend to be resurrected when we ourselves become parents or when we find ourselves in positions of authority over others – as teachers and managers. These drivers can be summarized as:

- 'Be perfect – like I want you to be.'
- 'Please me – by doing those things that I want you to do.'
- 'Try hard – to be the way I want you to be.'
- 'Be strong – by concealing the emotions that make it painful for you.'
- 'Hurry up – do it when I want you to, not when you do.'

The sting in these messages is one of conditionality – 'If you do these things and become the way I want you to be, then I'll love you.'

These drivers are signalled from one person to another by a distinctive set of words, tones, gestures, postures and facial expressions. We become so accustomed to them that a mere sigh is enough to trigger off the conflict between giving the other what they want and receiving approval or sustaining our own sense of unique selfness and receiving disapproval. These drivers are essentially the Theory X messages that attempt to condition and control the behaviour of others. Because they so often come from people whose love and approval we need we experience the management of our own reactions and responses as an intense and often painful struggle. Those who attempt to adopt a more life enhancing Theory Y approach to parenting, teaching and managing often encounter inner conflicts as the tension between our habitual patterns and our ideal behaviours are worked out. Under stress the drivers can dominate, and breakdown in professional relationships often occurs when the emerging drivers begin to clash with each other.

Achieving the 'unconditional positive regard' considered by Rogers to be so vital to the creation of the safe psychological climate for growth and change can seem an impossible challenge. Our humanity depends upon our capacity to recognize habits and patterns and the effects they have on others but we must never censor our strong and deep feelings, for as Rogers also points out, the helper also needs to engage in genuine behaviour. We should not be surprised when our interpersonal behaviour sometimes triggers off in others the painful emotions they have experienced when they were urged to be perfect and obedient, nor when the behaviours of others trigger them off in ourselves. These are the dynamics of the complex interpersonal world of the workplace and it is vital to be aware of them.

For too long we have contrived to keep the personal and professional apart. In most peoples' lives the two aspects of being are inextricably linked and connected. Professionalism is not about separating ourselves from who we are and becoming the role expected of us, but about integrating the essence of ourselves into the roles and responsibilities that we need to undertake. Theory X organizations are the ones which institutionalize the drivers of Transactional Analysis into the rules and regulations that prescribe and control behaviour. No wonder the cry so often heard is – 'They treat us like children here.' In other words the behaviour of managers triggers off those painful emotions we experienced as children when parents and teachers drove us to be other than we really were.

Effective leadership requires an almost heroic sensitivity to the inner worlds of colleagues. Blake and Mouton (1981) recognized many years ago that success in leadership is achieved when there is a proper balance between concern for the task and consideration for the people. In developing this respect for the individuality of others it is useful to consider the issue of rights and responsibilities. The struggle for rights and freedoms is an important part of our social and political history. It is a process of transforming the locus of control in society, organizations and individuals themselves. A proper balance between rights and responsibilities is by no means easy to achieve but remains one of the continuing challenges of management and leadership. Increasing trust involves a consequent decrease in control, as was observed in Chapter 5. Increasing the rights of individuals seldom produces an instant recognition that responsibility also has to increase to create a new balance. Accepting and exercising more personal and social responsibility comes if and when the psychological climate as well as the regulatory framework is trustful. Resolving the dynamic tension between Theory X and Theory Y requires patience and forebearance.

It is a matter of some debate what a charter of individual rights might look like, particularly in an organizational setting. Ann Dickson (1982) has offered the following:

1 to state personal needs and set personal priorities
2 to be treated with respect
3 to express personal feelings
4 to express opinions and values
5 to say 'yes' or 'no' on your own behalf
6 to make mistakes
7 to change your mind

 8 to say you do not understand
 9 to ask for what you want
10 to deal with others without requiring their approval

An open and collaborative working team could use a list such as this to explore and negotiate their own set of rights but also to generate the sorts of responsibilities and behaviours that team members would need to adopt to sustain them. This particular set provides much useful material for discussion and deliberation. Working the rights into a framework of self examination helps to tune into our own deepest feelings about personhood, responsibility and freedom and to generate strategies for the daily practice of leadership.

 1 How can I help and encourage my colleagues to express their needs and set personal priorities for themselves?
 2 In what specific ways do I demonstrate respect for my colleagues? What would each of them say about the nature and quality of the respect I extend?
 3 To what extent do I disclose my own personal feelings to others? How do I encourage others to be open and disclosing? How do I honour and respect confidentiality?
 4 What formal structures do I create for people to express opinions about their experiences within the organization? How well do we manage disagreement and misunderstanding?
 5 To what extent do I censor my own feelings when I say 'yes' or 'no', and how much is it to do with the need for approval and recognition?
 6 How do we handle our mistakes?
 7 What do I do when I have made a decision that was wrong and I need to change my mind?
 8 In what ways do I seek clarification and search for understanding?
 9 How do I ask for what I want?
10 In what ways do I separate my own needs from the needs of the organization when I deal with others?

An open and enhancing organizational culture is achieved when considerations such as these are given attention in a spirit of open-minded creativity. Ground rules for collaboration is probably a better way of defining rights and responsibilities and they need to be tried out, reviewed and amended as necessary. Successes as well as difficulties need to be noted and built on.

The issue of assumptions and their power to condition behaviour and performance in organizations has been a constant theme throughout this book. Building effective management cultures involves the critical examination of assumptions and their reconstruction as guiding principles and values. It is vital to challenge the taken for granted nature of many of the beliefs about organizational life. In a world of change this needs to become a regular process rather than an isolated event.

Leaders need to keep their assumptions under constant review – staying alert to the incidents of daily life that both confirm and challenge them. Assumptions are closely connected with our belief and value systems and are a fundamental part of our personal and professional identity. The process of becoming requires that the link between our assumptions and behaviours is constantly reviewed. Consistency between the two will build confidence in others and develop trust just as habitually saying one thing then doing another breeds resentment and diminishes trust and self-responsibility.

Since so many of our assumptions are taken for granted, it is useful to offer some for consideration and discussion. The following set provide an essentially Theory Y approach to leadership. They are not offered for indiscriminate adoption but as the basis for critical examination:

1 We are all individual and creative agents of change.
2 Each of us brings a unique set of experiences, understandings, values, skills and qualities as a rich resource for the organization.
3 We are all born with a powerful capacity for self-direction and self fulfilment. This capacity has often been crushed and inhibited during the process of childhood and education and may have been repressed in authoritarian organizations.
4 Our directional tendency can be reactivated in organizations if the right psychological climate for change and development can be created.
5 Such a capacity is created when senior managers behave in ways which enhance the organizational climate for change and help to build in individuals feelings of acceptance, belonging, involvement and achievement.
6 These leadership behaviours involve a willingness to trust people at all levels to demonstrate their capacity to be capable of doing more than the job asks of them.

Another set is offered by Ballard (1982):

1 People are constituted not bad, at least neutral and probably good.
2 The seeds of growth are inside people.
3 People can always do more than they are presently doing to become more than they presently are.
4 Each of us can be nicer to herself/himself than she/he tends to be.
5 Each of us is, in the end, alone and responsible.
6 We are always choosing our own lives.
7 Fear is our major limiter.
8 Human behaviour arises out of needs.
9 Awareness brings responsibility.
10 Listening is uniquely powerful in building awareness.

Leadership is essentially a process of developing organizational health, of creating the best possible human environment for people to work in. A healthy organization is one which copes with ailments and minor accidents and which can also face serious illness with optimism and courage. It is also one which keeps fit, takes regular exercise and pays attention to its diet.

A touch of quality

Total Quality Management (TQM) has arrived on the scene in a flurry of activity and excitement. In a world desperate for solutions to increasing confusion, new bandwagons have a seductive attraction about them. Developed first through the idea of quality assurance – formal undertakings about the specifications of a product or service – it has now reached out into most spheres of life and customer guarantees are now interpreted loftily in the concept of the Citizen's Charter while many organizations are seeking the endorsement of British Standard 5750 to give formal approval to their management processes. There is something of a competitive stampede about this latest management novelty as if its mere adoption will bring about success.

Despite the bandwagon tendency there is much about the concept of quality that reflects many of the themes explored in this book and contributes to the shifting nature of the management paradigm. Organizations that introduce TQM as a visible and high profile strategy may run the risk of failing to understand the essentially human scale nature of the quality concept and fail to grasp some of its fundamental ideas and key principles.

Quality assurance was conceived of as a means of underwriting the contractual relationship between an organization and its clients or customers. This requires attention to the interface between the organization and its external environment. In education this involves relationships with parents and the community; the sharing of aims and aspirations for pupils and their learning; and the presentation and explanation of outcomes and results. A more subtle principle of the quality concept is the idea that organizations also have a network of internal customers and suppliers – complex chains of givers and receivers – and it is to these that quality considerations need to be applied. The pursuit of a collaborative management culture is an elaboration of this principle, seeking to build powerful relationships of service and trust between the participants in the corporate exercise – between pupils and teachers, between the pupils themselves and between the various partners in the management of the school. It is the pursuit of interdependence and the recognition that is in the way that we give and take in the daily process of work that quality most importantly resides. If we can offer a quality service to our colleagues and pupils then we need have no fear that our outcomes will be unsatisfactory.

Allied to this is another principle – that quality needs to be in the process rather than the product. Quality assurance often involves a sophisticated and rigorous inspection of outcomes and end results. Yet inspecting outcomes is often wasteful – it only tends to tell you whether the processes designed to produce particular outcomes are effective or otherwise. A more important quality focus is that of the processes themselves. It is what we do day in and day out that counts and how individuals bring to their own specific roles and responsibilities a concern for quality and excellence.

Quality management is built on the idea that anything can be made better than it currently is and on the notion that there is no such thing as an insignificant improvement. This suggests that no part of the management process is too small for concern or attention and indeed it is in attention to small details that the key to success often lies. For too many organizations change involves grand gestures and fundamental restructuring. The more successful approach often lies along the path of improving in small and subtle ways what is already good and successful.

A further key principle is the recognition that quality itself exists in the experience of the user of a product or service. Quality is what the client or customer says it is, not what the producer wants to believe it is. For too long there has been a contentment with the idea that customers should merely approve of the product or have a sense of satisfaction. In the pursuit of quality nothing less than delight is enough. Somerset Maugham once remarked that only mediocre people are always at their best. It is not too difficult to provide a satisfactory service or make an average product. There is now a climate developing in which the expectations of the quality of experience are being raised. Increasingly people are feeling that the past has sold them short.

Since the management process is the key focus and quality is achieved by giving attention to the internal relationships of giving and receiving then we can isolate five particular aspects for consideration.

Quality of involvement

This concerns the extent to which the partners in the management of the school experience a real sense of involvement in the process. Delight can be experienced when there is a collective sense of collaboration and a strong personal identification of each team member with the ideas, visions and plans of the school. Delight can also be experienced when there is a strong sense of collective commitment and a genuine sharing in both the successes and disappointments of the management enterprises.

Quality of communication

This is achieved when there is a high measure of shared understanding about policies, plans, procedures and processes, and where there is a determination to press for clarity of meaning, to test out differences of interpretation and to grapple with ambiguities. Everyone needs to feel a personal sense of responsibility to the collective understanding of the team and a high level of checking out and a determination not to make hasty assumptions or draw quick conclusions is also required.

Quality of interactions

It is in the interpersonal transactions of daily life that the key to quality lies. Each and every management interaction is an opportunity to achieve quality. It lies in the sensitivity with which we respond to the needs of colleagues, the clarity and directness of our requests to them and the appreciation and delight we express when quality is experienced. Each interaction is an opportunity to push for excellence.

Quality of initiative

This is the extent to which individuals exercise personal acts of initiative in the pursuit of quality. It requires a determination not to miss any opportunity to make a small but significant improvement and quality is often best experienced in the small detail. Much will depend on the extent to which senior managers cultivate a climate of trust and an internal locus of control in members of the management partnership.

Quality of responses to challenge

One of the best tests of quality is the way that people respond to external and internal challenges and their individual and collective capacity to engage in creative thinking and take decisions about the future. Challenge is an opportunity to put quality to the test, to stretch commitments and competencies and to extend the sense of achievement that is experienced when a team works really well together.

Developing a high quality management culture depends upon a collective aptitude in a number of important areas.

Creative insight

This involves looking below the surface features of organizational issues to the core, checking assumptions, asking lots of questions and delving into causes and consequences. It stems from a keen curiosity about how the organization works and how it can be improved. Team meetings will be searches for truth, exchanges of perceptions and rehearsals of possibilities.

quality shows that people will pay more for it. In schools this means that pupils will invest considerably more effort and involvement if the learning experiences offered them bring appropriate challenge, support and delight. It has also shown that quality is not necessarily expensive. In some organizations when quality has gone up, costs have gone down. This is particularly so when the participants in the organization are enabled to see that it is their contribution, rather than capital investment which is the significant factor in achieving excellence. Working in quality minded organizations has also been found to be stimulating and invigorating, because quality is not something that is insisted upon or required through regulation. It is something that individuals develop a commitment to when they feel fully engaged and involved at all levels of the management process, capable of exercising responsibility, sharing in decision making and operating with a high degree of personal autonomy. It has also been found that experiencing delight, both within the organization and outside it has a multiplying effect which increases loyalty, commitment, self-respect and reputation.

Comfort in chaos

When Tom Peters wrote *Thriving on Chaos* in 1987 he was anxious to help leaders and managers acclimatize themselves to a changing world characterized by relentless pace, turbulence and discontinuity. He described the manager of the future as one who was comfortable in confusion and creative in crisis. The process of becoming is not a discrete act of professional development to achieve these qualities but a continuous process of reaching into the future, acquiring new knowledge and building new competencies.

In this state of increased complexity it is tempting to conclude that the management of change is about keeping up with the external environment – a sort of obedient adaptation. This is to assume an external locus of control, to accept that in the world of change it is those outside the school who set the pace, create the conditions and determine the agenda. However, it is the way that we manage the relationship with an unstable and changing environment that really counts and how we seize opportunities to advance individual and organizational visions and aspirations. Changed circumstances create new possibilities, present fresh perspectives, offer different angles and open up undiscovered pathways. Being alert to the external environment is not only about anticipating difficulty, noting potential problems but also about scanning for new growth points, forming new connections and spotting opportunities. But managing change is far from simply being a case of spotting the trends and adapting to keep pace. There is as much need for individuality, flair and leadership as there has ever been. The visions have to be sustained but they may have to be sharper, the structures to achieve them more flexible and more responsive to change, but it will be the creative acts of individuals, passionately connected to the cause of schools and learning, that will exercise the most profound influence on development in the turbulent years ahead.

Claiming a pioneering role for the individual organization is a vital and proper part of leadership. Successful ways of educating will be discovered by schools themselves, not achieved by legislation or regulation. Part of the process of change needs to be an increased belief in the integrity of individual schools to be their own agents of change. Two perspectives are of particular interest in the process of balancing the needs of a changing external environment with the visions and intentions of the individual organization.

The first perspective is provided by Gareth Morgan who in *Images of Organization* (1986) examines a range of metaphors through which we can come to a deeper understanding of organizations and their dynamics. Among the metaphors he explores are organizations as machines, as organisms, as brains, as cultures, as political systems, as psychic prisons, as flux and transformation and as instruments of domination. This multiperspective approach to the study of organizations opens up new structures for analysis and creates new opportunities for understanding.

In his consideration of organization as flux and transformation, Morgan presses the notion of the egocentric organization – one that has a somewhat fixed and self centred notion of who it is and a determination to sustain that identity come what may. Like the 'defender' position described by Miles and Snow the egocentric organization has a certain arrogance and conceit in the face of pressure to modify and adapt. On the other hand, there are organizations which are sometimes too eager and willing to sacrifice their own integrity in the pursuit of approval. In an attempt to offer such a creative way through this polarized dilemma, Morgan refers to the theory of autopoiesis – the capacity of living systems to self-create and self-renew. The theory attempts to challenge the view that the way that organisms evolve depends on the forces and pressures exerted by the external environment. It suggests a set of interdependent relationships between organisms and their surroundings in which neither the organism itself, nor the environment in which it exists, is dominant, but in which the organism has the power to sustain its integrity and establish its own identity.

One of the key challenges for schools is how to establish such a relationship of interdependence with a turbulent and fast changing educational environment. The theory of autopoiesis helps in a number of ways. First, it helps us to see that organizations are essentially self-creating, self-organizing and constantly attempting to achieve a distinctive identity in harmony with the environment. In other words, the capacity to be distinctive but also to fit in. Secondly, it helps us to appreciate that many of the problems of development and change are not so much to do with external pressures but with the internal struggle to maintain the distinctive identity in which individual and collective energy is invested. Thirdly, it helps us to see that in adjusting to a fast changing world an organization must give primary attention to the factors that shape its own distinctive self-identity and consequently its relationship with the wider world.

While sensitivity of response to the forces and pressures exerted in the external environment is a key function of leadership it is attention to the forces and pressures within that enables progress to be made and transformation to be achieved.

The second perspective is that of chaos itself. Traditional science has tended to concentrate on predictability and explaining the whole in terms of its distinctive and separate parts. In recent years some scientists and mathematicians have delved into the nature of random complexity in search of hidden patterns of order. Chaos theory has emerged to explain that pattern and order exist in systems that were previously considered unstable, random and unpredictable. Study of many varied systems such as climate, the patterns of spiralling smoke and the rhythms of heartbeats has revealed that although the exact course of apparently chaotic systems cannot be predicted, the constraints on their behaviour can. Among the fascinating discoveries have been how complex systems change and undergo transformation often through small and apparently insignificant change in one part of the system having an effect on the wider system out of all proportion to its size. The example often quoted is the flapping of a butterfly wing in California having an impact on turbulent weather conditions over Japan.

Many people will recall numerous occasions in organizational life when apparently insignificant events – a dispute between two colleagues for example – has created an effect out of all proportion. Teachers too will know how the behaviour of a single pupil can significantly alter the social dynamics of a class.

There are important messages here for the management of change. First, we need to learn not to be too surprised at the capacity of small incidents and events to create turbulence. In fact quality is built on the idea that excellence resides in sensitive attention to the small but significant aspects of change. Secondly, we need to develop a sensitivity to details within the systemic whole. Thirdly, we need to develop a new level of cause and effect consciousness – spotting small changes in organizational behaviour and looking for their enlarged consequences elsewhere in the system.

As organizations have become more complex they have also seemed to become more chaotic, with predictable patterns more deeply buried. Crisis management has become a way of life and confusion and uncertainty have created discomfort and stress. But it is no use grieving over a world that is past. If we know that hidden patterns of order exist we can learn to spot causal connections between apparently unrelated parts of the organizational system and to tease out the nature of these connections. Leadership becomes a process of tuning into the complex rhythms and harmonies of organizational life. It is less about wanting to recreate the world in our own image and getting things the way we want them and more about making connections, creating conditions and building opportunities.

Managing change in schools is a never-ending challenge. The risks may seem greater and the tasks more demanding but the rewards for success and achievement more profound. Those currently occupying senior posts in schools, and those to follow them in the next few years, are essentially a generation of pioneers faced with managing the paradigm shift and creating new management strategies to guide schools into a changed and changing future.

Bibliography

Adair, J. (1983) *Effective Leadership*, London: Pan.

Adair, J. (1987) *Not Bosses but Leaders*, London: Kogan Page.

Argyris, C. (1964) *Integrating the Individual and the Organization*, Chichester: Wiley.

Argyris, C. and Schön, D. (1974) *Theory in Practice: Increasing Professional Effectiveness*, San Francisco: Jossey-Bass.

Ballard, J. (1982) *Circlebook*, New York: Irvington.

Blake, R. R. and Mouton, J. S. (1981) *The Versatile Manager: A Grid Profile*, Irwin Dorsey.

Blanchard, K., Zigarmi, P. and Zigarmi, D. (1988) *Leadership and the One Minute Manager*, London: Fontana/Collins.

Blanchard, K., Oncken, W. and Burrows, H. (1990) *The One Minute Manager Meets the Monkey*, London: Fontana/Collins.

Bohm, D. (1980) *Wholeness and the Implicate Order*, London: Routledge & Kegan Paul.

Bolam, R. (1990) 'Recent developments in England and Wales' in Joyce, B. M. (ed.) *Changing School Culture through Staff Development – 1990 Yearbook of the Association for Supervision and Curriculum Development*, Virginia: ASCD.

Boulding, E. (1988) *Building a Global Civic Culture: Education for an Interdependent World*, New York: Teachers College Press.

Buzan, T. (1982) *Use Your Head*, London: Ariel Books/BBC Books.

Capra, F. (1983) *The Turning Point*, London: Flamingo.

Coulson, A. (1985) 'The fear of change', unpublished paper.

Day, C. and Baskett, H. K. (1982) 'Discrepancies between intentions and practice: re-examining some basic assumptions about adult and continuing professional education', *International Journal of Lifelong Education*, 1(2): 143–55.

Day, C., Whitaker, P. and Wren, D. (1987) *Appraisal and Professional Development in Primary Schools*, Milton Keynes: Open University Press.

Dickens, C. (1961) *Hard Times*, London: Collins.

Dickson, A. (1982) *A Woman in her Own Right*, London: Quartet.

Elliott, J. (1977) 'Conceptualising relationships between research/evaluation procedures and in-service teacher education', *British Journal of In-service Education*, 4(2).

Eraut, M. E. (1977) 'Strategies for promoting teacher development', *British Journal of In-service Education*, 1(1 and 2).

Erikson, E. (1977) *Childhood and Society*, London: Triad/Granada.

Ferguson, M. (1982) *The Aquarian Conspiracy*, London: Granada.

Fullan, M. and Hargreaves, A. (1992) *What's Worth Fighting for in Your School?*, Buckingham: Open University Press.

Garratt, B. (1987) *The Learning Organization*, London: Fontana/Collins.

Gray, H. L. (1987) 'A perspective on organization theory' in Westoby, A. (ed.) *Culture and Power in Educational Organizations*, Milton Keynes: Open University Press.

Handy, C. (1976) *Understanding Organizations*, London: Penguin.

Handy, C. (1990) *Inside Organizations*, London: BBC Books.

Handy, C. and Aitken, R. (1986) *Understanding Schools as Organizations*, London: Penguin.

Heller, H. (1985) *Helping Schools Change*, York: Centre for Study of Comprehensive Schools.

Herzberg, F. (1966) *Work and the Nature of Man*, New York: Staple Press.

Hicks, D. (1993) *Education for the Future: A Practical Classroom Guide* (forthcoming), Godalming: World Wide Fund for Nature.

Holt, J. (1971) *The Underachieving School*, London: Penguin.

Holt, J. (1973) *Freedom and Beyond*, London: Penguin.

Hopson, B. and Scally, M. (1981) *Lifeskills Teaching*, London: McGraw-Hill.

Johnson, G. and Scholes, K. (1989) *Exploring Corporate Strategy*, Hemel Hempstead: Prentice-Hall.

Knowles, M. (1983) 'Androgogy: an emerging technology for adult learning' in Tight, M. (ed.) *Adult Learning and Education*, London: Croom Helm.

Koestler, A. (1978) *Janus*, London: Hutchinson.

Kolb, D. (1984) *Experiential Learning: Experience as the Source of Learning and Development*, Englewood Cliffs, NJ: Prentice-Hall.

Kolb, D. A., Rubin, I. M. and McIntyre, J. M. (1971) *Organizational Psychology: An Experiential Approach*, Hemel Hempstead: Prentice-Hall.

Kuhn, T. (1970) *The Structure of Scientific Revolutions*, Chicago: University of Chicago Press.

Laing, R. D. (1967) *The Politics of Experience*, London: Penguin.

Leithwood, K. A. (1990) 'The principal's role in teacher development' in Joyce, B. M. (ed.) *Changing School Culture through Staff Development – Yearbook of the Association for Supervision and Curriculum Development*, Virginia: ASCD.

Lewin, K. (1936) *Principles of Topological Psychology*, New York: McGraw-Hill.

Lieberman, M. and Hardie, M. (1981) *Resolving Family and other Conflicts*, Santa Cruz: Unity Press.

Luft, J. (1969) *Of Human Interaction*, Palo Alto: National Press Books.

McGregor, D. (1960) *The Human Side of Enterprise*, New York: McGraw-Hill.

Mant, A. (1985) *Leaders We Deserve*, Oxford: Blackwell.

Maslow, A. (1970) *Motivation and Personality*, New York: Harper & Row.

Milbrath, L. (1989) *Envisioning A Sustainable Society: Learning Our Way Out*, Albany: State University of New York Press.

Miles, R. E. and Snow, C. C. (1978) *Organization Strategy, Structure and Process*, New York: McGraw-Hill.

Miller, A. (1987a) *For Your Own Good*, London: Virago.

Miller, A. (1987b) *The Drama of Being A Child*, London: Virago.

Minzberg, H. (1973) *The Nature of Managerial Work*, New York: Harper & Row.

Morgan, G. (1986) *Images of Organization*, Newbury Park: SAGE.

Morgan, G. (1989) *Creative Organization Theory*, Newbury Park: SAGE.

Murgatroyd, S. (1988) 'Consulting as counselling: the theory and practice of structural consulting' in Gray, H. L. (ed.) *Management Consultancy in Schools*, London: Cassell.

Nias, J., Southworth, G. and Yeomans, R. (1989) *Staff Relations in the Primary School*, London: Cassell.

Papert, S. (1980) *Mindstorms – Children, Computers and Powerful Ideas*, Brighton: Harvester Press.

Peters, T. (1988) *Thriving on Chaos*, London: Macmillan.

Peters, T. and Waterman, R. (1982) *In Search of Excellence*, New York: Harper & Row.

Peters, T. and Austin, N. (1986) *A Passion for Excellence*, London: Fontana/Collins.

Phares, J. (1976) *Locus of Control in Personality*, New Jersey: General Learning Press.

Plant, R. (1987) *Managing Change and Making it Stick*, London: Fontana.

Postle, D. (1989) *The Mind Gymnasium*, London: Macmillan.

Revens, R. W. (1982) *The Origins and Growth of Action Learning*, Chartwell-Bratt: Bromley & Lund.

Richardson, R. (1976) *Learning for Change in World Society*, London: World Studies Project.

Robertson, J. (1983) *The Sane Alternative*, Ironbridge: James Robertson.

Rogers, C. (1967) *On Becoming a Person*, London: Constable.

Rotter, J. R. (1981) 'Generalized expectancies for internal versus external control of reinforcement' in Hopson, B. and Scally, M. *Teaching Life Skills*, London: McGraw-Hill.

Schein, E. H. (1980) *Organizational Psychology*, Hemel Hempstead: Prentice-Hall.

Schön, D. (1983) *The Reflective Practitioner: How Professionals Think in Action*, London: Temple Smith.

Senge, P. (1990) *The Fifth Discipline*, London: Century Business.

Singer, B. D. (1974) 'The future focused role image' in Toffler, A. *Learning for Tomorrow: the Role of the Future in Education*, New York: Random House.

Toffler, A. (1971) *Future Shock*, London: Pan.

Toffler, A. (1980) *The Third Wave*, London: Collins.

Weick, K. E. (1988) 'Educational organizations as loosely coupled systems' in Westoby, A. (ed.) *Culture and Power in Educational Organizations*, Milton Keynes: Open University Press.

Westoby, A. (ed.) (1988) *Culture and Power in Educational Organizations*, Milton Keynes: Open University Press.

Whitaker, P. (1983) *The Primary Head*, London: Heinemann Educational Books.

Whitehead, A. (1931) 'Introduction' in Wallace, B. *Business Adrift*, New York: McGraw-Hill.

Index

Dfu-02548

2/984